The Sacraments

Seán Swayne (Ed.)

The Sacraments

Pastoral Directory
of the Irish Episcopal Conference.

Veritas Publications Dublin 1976

First published 1976 by
Veritas Publications
7/8 Lr. Abbey Street, Dublin.

This edition 1977

© 1976 Irish Episcopal Conference.
Set in 10/11 pt Plantin.

Printed and bound in the Republic of Ireland
by Cahill (1976) Limited, Dublin.

Designed by Liam Miller.
Cover by Steven Hope.

Cover illustration is based on the lower knop of the Lismore crozier.

The following assisted the Episcopal Conference in the preparation of
this *Directory*:
Miss Margaret Daly, Sister Kathleen Delaney, Father Brian Gogan,
CSSp, Father Brendan Houlihan, Father Seán McEntee, Father
Patrick McGoldrick, Father Ray Moloney, SJ, Father Timothy
O'Connor, Father Joseph Quinn, Father Martin Slattery, Father Seán
Swayne, Father Jeremiah Threadgold, Father Liam Walsh, OP.

ISBN 0-905092-13-9
CAT. NO. 3342

Contents

Introduction

The Sacraments: A Pastoral Directory is likely to prove an inestimable boon to priests. Few things are more important in the life of the Church today than the worthy celebration of the liturgy. In the liturgy Christ is present *and acting* in his Church. "By his power he is present in the sacraments" says the Second Vatican Council "so that when anybody baptises it is really Christ himself who baptises." It is obviously of supreme importance that the sacred liturgical actions, by their own dignity and beauty and by the way in which they are performed, should reflect and, in a sense, point to, the supernatural realities which lie beneath them. Worthily celebrated the liturgy can preach Christ in a way that goes deeper than the formal sermon or homily.

The great renewal of liturgical rites which was initiated by the Second Vatican Council provides a wealth of material to achieve these ends. As yet, however, this material is diffused in a multitude of official documents and there has been a great need for a single book which would collate all this in easily accessible form. This *Directory* does this but it is much more than a "Code" of liturgical law. It summarizes the principles and norms of the new liturgy of the sacraments but at the same time it enriches this material with suggestions and comments of a pastoral character, designed to help priests grasp the thinking which lies behind the new rites. While it is primarily designed for priests, lay people also will find it very helpful. It should serve as an excellent book for Study Groups and conferences. I gladly wish it every success.

Archbishop of Armagh
Primate of All Ireland

31 August 1976

1 Baptism

BAPTISM OF INFANTS

Preparation

a] Parish community

The Christian community must know what it is doing when it celebrates the sacrament of Baptism. Its members must know what the ritual has done for themselves, and what it has to offer those who come to be baptised. They need to be regularly instructed on the subject. Apart from ensuring that the subject is dealt with adequately in schools, priests should preach on it at least once each year. Lent is a particularly appropriate time for doing so and the readings of the lenten Masses, particularly on Sundays 3, 4, 5, provide an excellent basis for a baptismal catechesis. The renewal of baptismal vows either at the end of lenten retreats or more particularly at the Easter Vigil should come as the climax of baptismal instruction.

Sacramental theology of the Church has developed considerably in recent years. To preach well on Baptism, to understand and explain the restored liturgy of the sacrament, priests will need to have kept up with these developments. The *Constitution on the Liturgy* of Vatican II, and the *General Instruction on Baptism* given in the new rituals of the sacrament will be their best guide. Among the truths about Baptism that need to be emphasised are (1) that Baptism is a personal act of Christ, inviting others to share in his Paschal Mystery; (2) that the significance of the ritual comes from the biblical background about the role of water in the history of man's salvation; (3) that the negative effect of the sacrament — removal of original sin — has to be seen in the positive context of initiation into the grace and holiness of Christ through membership of the Church and the right to participate in its community life and sacramental celebrations; (4) that Baptism has value for infants, but that because it is the sacrament of faith it can only be given (outside danger of death) to those who have a reasonable prospect of continuing formation in the faith.

Attendance *(Intro. 4)*

A successful catechesis on Baptism should have made it clear that the local church is responsible for what happens at the Baptism of new members. Parishioners should not be surprised when they are invited and encouraged to attend the regular celebration of Baptism. The invitation should be addressed firstly to the family, relatives, neighbours and friends of the child to be baptised. Such a circle of people gather together readily enough in church for weddings and funerals. There is all the more reason why they should do so for Baptism. The wider parish community should also be encouraged to attend, at least occasionally during the year. They will be there to welcome a new member to their community, to pray for that new member, to grow in appreciation of their own Baptism, and to perform an act of devotion that can do everything for them that traditional forms of "evening devotions" were intended to do.

Since it is Baptism that gives one the right and power to take part in all the other sacraments it is desirable that people who are preparing for some of the other sacraments should have the sense of their own Baptism renewed by attendance at a parish Baptism. Children who are about to be confirmed might be asked to come to a special celebration at which they would be reminded of their own Baptism and its connection with their Confirmation. People about to be married might also be encouraged to attend.

Place and time *(Intro. 8-14)*

Baptism initiates a child into the local Christian community. The obvious place to celebrate it, then, is the church in which the local community meets for its liturgy. If people understand this and accept that Baptism is not just a private family celebration they will be less likely to ask for Baptism in another church or place of their own choice.

There are good practical reasons for having the celebration of Baptism at a fixed time each week or month. Apart from being convenient for the priest it will facilitate the faithful who may wish to attend. When a number of children are baptised together on these occasions the gathering of different families and their friends enhances the community character of the celebration. But priests in larger parishes will be aware that if the group is too large it will be difficult to pay proper attention to each family and their child. There should not be more than ten children, even if this means arranging a second celebration of the sacrament each week *(Gen. Intro. 27)*.

Because Sunday is the day when the Church is most conscious of the paschal mystery of Christ it is the most appropriate day of the week for celebrating Baptism. It is also the day when the faithful can most easily attend. Baptism may be celebrated during Sunday Mass. The community gathered in eucharistic assembly is certainly the ideal setting for the welcoming of new members into the Body of Christ. But because the combination of Baptism and Eucharist makes special demands on the time and concentration of the faithful this can be done only on special occasions and after due notice and preparation.

The most perfect setting for Baptism is undoubtedly the celebration of the Easter Vigil. The Paschal Mystery is then re-enacted in the fullest possible way and the faithful who are present are generally disposed better than at any other time to play their part in its celebration through Baptism. The grace that is available to the whole community on such an occasion is too precious to lightly put aside because of the admitted but relatively minor difficulties that it can cause parents and priests.

To ensure that the local community is made aware of its responsibilities it will be well for the priest to remind his people from time to time of the arrangements for Baptism, and to encourage them to attend. To pray for the newly baptised, even by name, each Sunday in the Prayer of the Faithful is also a valuable way of associating the people with this important event in the life of their church.

b] Parents *(Intro. 5)*

Parents should be encouraged to contact the priest about the Baptism of their child "as soon as possible, and even before the child is born" *(Intro. 8,2)*. The priest will want to meet them, preferably by visiting their home, to prepare them pastorally for their part in Baptism. There is more to be done than simply arranging the date and time. If parents are to play an active part in the Baptism of their child they will usually have to be instructed in the rite. In telling them what they have to do the priest will try to convey the meaning of the rite and prepare them to become spiritually involved in it. If, as the Ritual recommends, *(Gen. Intro. 34, Intro. 7,2)*, they can be given some choice about even minor details of the ceremony they will be more likely to participate actively in it. And if the priest prays with the family during such meetings they will undoubtedly be better prepared to play their full spiritual part in the sacrament *(Intro. 27)*.

Sometimes the priest will need to satisfy himself about the parents' motivation in asking Baptism for their child. It can no longer be automatically assumed that all parents have correct attitudes to the sacrament and that they are capable of providing the requisite Christian formation for their child. The quality of their own Christian life and the regularity of their sacramental practice will tell more than their words *(Gen. Intro. 3; Intro. 8,4; 25)*. Parents should be encouraged to give a Christian baptismal name to the child, or at least one which has a Christian meaning.

In arranging the *date and time* of Baptism the priest will emphasise the positive value of uniting the child to Christ in his Church as soon as possible. It is in this way, rather than by playing on the fears of the parents for their child's salvation that he will encourage them to avoid undue delay and yet at the same time satisfy them that they should wait, for a few weeks if necessary, so that the Baptism can be more fittingly celebrated in the church, in the presence of both parents, with members of the family and friends. Delays for any other motives, or simply out of carelessness should be discouraged *(Intro. 8)*.

Parents may need some guidance about their choice of *godparents (Gen. Intro. 8-10)*. They should be reminded that godparents "speak for" the child in church and take some responsibility for its Christian formation. They must not only be people whose word can be taken seriously but also people whose right to "sponsor" a new member for the Church comes from the fact that they themselves are already fully initiated members. If the role of godparents is explained in this way people should be able to understand more readily the legal stipulations of the Church about them.

Godparents should:
(1) be mature enough to undertake this responsibility;
(2) have received the three sacraments of initiation: Baptism, Confirmation and the Eucharist;
(3) be a member of the Catholic Church, canonically free to carry out this office. *(Gen. Intro. 10)*.

A member of a separated Eastern Church may act as godparent along with a Catholic godparent *(ATE 48)*.

A Christian of another communion can be admitted with a Catholic godparent *as a Christian witness* of the baptism *(ATE 57)*.

c] Ministers *(Gen. Intro. 11-15; Intro. 7)*

Because Baptism is the reception of children into the local church the normal minister of the sacrament should be one of the *priests* responsible for that church. It is a ministry that should not be lightly delegated. If a family wishes a priest relative or friend to have a part in the ceremony it could be suggested that he would assist the local priest in the parish Baptism and do the actual baptising of their child *(Rite 60)*. If, however, he is to perform the entire ceremony it is preferable that he should do the regular parish Baptism rather than have a quasi-private ceremony for one family. In that case it is desirable that one of the local priests should also be present.

Deacons may also be invited to perform the sacrament, particularly if they are doing regular pastoral work in the parish. The solemnity of the sacrament is increased if the priest and deacon officiate together, each performing his proper ministry. Apart from generally assisting the priest the deacon will have his normal role in the liturgy of the word (which may include giving the homily) and where there are several children he may anoint and baptise some of them *(Gen. Intro. 15; Rite 34)*.

Servers should also be trained to play their part, leading the various processions with cross and candles and serving the priest and deacon.

Because singing contributes so much to the celebration and helps to intensify the spirit of prayer, the musical resources of the parish should be employed as regularly as possible at Baptisms. The *organist and the choir* should have a repertoire of suitable hymns, and the parishioners might be taught to join in at least some of these *(Gen. Intro. 33)*.

The same reasons that persuade a priest to approach the Eucharist in a spirit of recollection and prayer should influence his preparation for the ministry of Baptism. In this sacrament he is going to make Christ present and bring about an outpouring of the Spirit. The effectiveness of his ministry, for his own sanctification no less than for that of his people, will be greatly increased by the sense of God that he brings to the celebration. Spending some moments in prayer before beginning will help him to make the Baptism a richer spiritual exercise for all who take part in it.

Choice of texts *(Gen. Intro. 34)*

The priest must decide in advance what texts he will use at those points of the ritual where choice is given. These alternative texts are meant to provide an opportunity for presenting the mystery of Baptism from different standpoints. They also allow the priest to adapt the celebration to the needs of different congregations. And they help him to escape the feeling of routine that can come from doing exactly the same thing each time he celebrates the sacrament. If he is to make his choice thoughtfully and on the basis not of expediency but of a real appreciation of the different possibilities (some suggestions on the value of the different alternatives will be given later), he will have to do it before the celebration begins.

Priest's own words

Some of the words given in the ritual are offered as examples of what might be said rather than as obligatory formulas. The celebrant is told he may say the same thing in his own words. These improvisations need to be planned in advance on the same basis as the choice of texts is made. They occur at:

Opening Dialogue *(Rite, 36-40, 74-77);*
Introduction to Sacrament *(52, 88);*
Introduction to Lord's Prayer *(67, 101).*

The priest may feel it necessary to add a few words of explanation and guidance here and there throughout the ceremony (although if the general catechesis of the sacrament is well done and the participants are properly prepared it is better to let the ceremony speak for itself). These interventions should be confined to the main "turning points" of the rite; they should be brief and prepared in advance.

Homily

The homily can make each celebration of the sacrament unique and alive by applying it to the particular situation of the group of people who are gathered there. It will only do this if it is prepared before each Baptism. Obviously there are certain general truths about the sacrament that may be repeated each time, and every priest will have his own favourite theological approach to the subject. But if these general ideas are to draw any given congregation into an understanding of the sacrament and an acceptance of the demands it makes on them they cannot be presented in stereotyped form. They have to be brought into focus by the priest's pastoral understanding of the needs of each congregation. This will only happen if he gives some thought to his homily before each Baptism.

Movement *(Gen. Intro. 24-26)*

The ritual stipulates that various stages of the sacrament should be celebrated in different parts of the church, and that there should be some form of procession from place to place. The layout of each church will determine to a certain extent how much of this is possible, and the size of the expected congregation will also be a factor. However, the significance of the different positions and the solemnity created by movement from one to another should encourage priests to devote some effort and ingenuity to making the most of their churches and, when necessary, overcoming their limitations. This will require some advance planning. A couple of patterns could be worked out to suit different circumstances. The church will then have to be arranged and the ministers and congregation directed according to the needs of the pattern chosen for each celebration.

Music *(Gen. Intro. 33)*

Depending on musical resources, hymns or chants will be chosen for:

1. Entrance
2. Responsorial Psalm
3. Alleluia and verse
4. Procession to the font
5. Acclamation after Baptism
6. Conclusion

Check-list of items required:
Vestments
Ritual
Lectionary
List of names
Register and certificates
Fresh water for font (heated)
Towel
Oils
Paschal candle
Candle for each child
Booklets for people

Celebration of Baptism

a] Reception of children *(Intro. 16)*

While the Rite sets down definite things that have to be done in this first stage of Baptism it allows great freedom about how they should be done and what words should be used. This is to encourage the priest to give a warm personal welcome to parents and to show some appreciation of the joy and pride they feel about their child. The enquiry about the name of the child and the touching of it with the sign of the cross are no less ordinary human reactions to a new baby for the fact that they are part of the sacrament. The informality of the priest's approach will not alone put parents at their ease but also help him to express the spiritual welcome the Church is offering in a way that is appropriate to each situation. He will be able to show the special delicacy that is required when, for example, the mother has died in giving birth to the child; or when the mother is widowed, or unmarried; or when the child is of an inter-Church marriage *(Intro. 31)*.

The welcome is more impressive and the informality more easily achieved if the children are received at the door of the church. If there is a large gathering of people for the ceremony

the parents and godparents might be asked to remain near the
door, while others go to their places. Once the reception has
been completed the parents will then be invited to come — if
possible in a procession led by cross and candle bearers — to
where the liturgy of the word is to be celebrated. Places can be
reserved for them there.

A baptismal hymn, sung while the ministers enter the church
and during the procession from the entrance to where the
liturgy of the word is being celebrated, will help to bind the
congregation together in an atmosphere of joy and prayer.

b] Celebration of God's word *(Intro. 17)*

The reading and preaching of God's word is meant to stimulate
the faith of the congregation and their acceptance of the
implications of Baptism. It is in this living faith of the Church
that the children are being baptised and from it they will in due
course draw their own faith. The priest will want to take full
advantage of the wide selection of readings offered in the
Lectionary (and not just of the few passages printed in the
Ritual) to awaken and instruct the baptismal faith of the people
who are present; he will endeavour to have the Responsorial
Psalm and Gospel acclamation sung; he will use the homily to
show the application of God's word to the real conditions of the
life he knows they lead. He will be aware that some of those
present may be weak in faith and commitment to the regular
practices of the Christian life, and will make a special effort to
recall them to fidelity.

The families of the children being baptised may be given
some choice in the readings to be used and may be invited to do
the actual reading.

The children may be taken to some place like a "crying
room" if it is felt they will disturb the liturgy of the word
(Intro. 14). If they are kept in the church their mothers, or
those who hold them, need not stand during the reading of the
gospel.

Because there is so much movement and activity during the

celebration of Baptism it is not always easy to cultivate the atmosphere of interior prayer which the fruitful celebration of any sacrament requires. The period of silence recommended by the Ritual after the homily would, if its purpose is explained to the people and its approximate length announced in advance, help them, and the priest also, to a more recollected, prayerful participation in the sacrament.

The variety and flexibility allowed in the intercessions and invocation of the saints give the priest another opportunity to adapt the sacrament to the real and local needs of his people.

c] Prayer of exorcism and anointing *(Intro. 17)*

The exorcism and anointing that conclude the preparatory section of the sacrament represent the withdrawing of the child from the forces of evil that threaten it in the world. Parents who are conscious of the threat which disease presents to the health of their children and who have them innoculated against such hazards should be disposed to understand these spiritually protective rituals. The moral hazards which they know their children will be surrounded by as they grow up will make them sensitive to the reality of evil and the power of Satan in the world. But it is ultimately their own faith in Christ and their own experience of the power of his grace in overcoming evil that will allow them to understand what the Church is praying for in this part of the ritual. Although the priest may use human analogies to explain exorcism and anointing he will be careful not to suggest that there is anything magical about the ritual. The power of Satan has indeed been broken by Christ. But it is in the continuing care of the Christian community and particularly of the parents themselves that the protection of Christ will be actually realised for these children.

d] Celebration of the sacrament *(Intro. 18)*

The build-up to this central moment of Baptism is intensified if there is a procession with music at this point to the baptistry, and if the baptistry is well laid out and appointed. However, if the congregation cannot be conveniently gathered in or around the baptistry it will be better to arrange a temporary font on or near the sanctuary, so that all can see the actual Baptism. This font should be solid and impressive, and careful thought should be given to its position and setting.

The increase in solemnity that should occur as the central part of the sacrament begins — corresponding somewhat to what happens at the beginning of the Eucharistic Prayer at Mass — depends very much on the attitude and behaviour of the priest as he asks the people to pray with him for the coming of divine life. The prayers over the water are among the most magnificent in the liturgy of the Church. They suppose an understanding of how the sacraments fit into the pattern of salvation history; of how the saving work of God was made visible through water in various events of the Old Testament, in the life of Christ, and now in the waters of Baptism; of how going "under" the water (if not by immersion at least by having it poured on the head) makes one die with Christ to sin, and how coming "out" of the water makes one rise with Christ, reborn in grace. These prayers make it clear that there is much more to Baptism than the washing away of original sin. People will only appreciate these ideas if they have been well instructed in the meaning of the sacrament. Indeed the text of these prayers over the water would be an excellent basis for a catechesis of the sacrament.

In choosing from the forms of this prayer given in the Ritual the priest will note that the first is the most comprehensive and supposes some appreciation of the Christian meaning of the Old Testament; the second and third use New Testament ideas only, the one praising the Persons of the Trinity in turn and appealing to each to carry out its proper work in the economy of man's salvation, the other following the same trinitarian pattern and drawing attention to the missionary call of those who are baptised.

It should be noted that even when the baptismal water has already been blessed, or when water consecrated at the Easter

Vigil is being used, the prayer is still said over it. Only a brief portion of it is omitted and that is replaced by another text.

Renunciation of sin and profession of faith

The rite of Baptism, as of all the sacraments, not alone makes Christ efficaciously present but also expresses the Church's response to his grace. It is in this encounter of the Church with Christ that grace is actually caused. Those who celebrate the sacrament are expected to make this response personally, and to ensure that those who are receiving the sacrament make it also. When parents and godparents present an infant for Baptism they are undertaking responsibility to pass on their own Christian attitudes to the child so that it can eventually respond fully to the grace of the sacrament. They express these attitudes in the Renunciation of Sin and The Profession of Faith.

Conversion from sin and faith in the Gospel of Christ are the two characteristic elements of the special response required for the grace of Baptism. The mysterious death to sin which Baptism brings about has to be matched by a personal moral choice to turn away from sin and everything that leads to it. And the mysterious life in Christ communicated by the sacrament has to be matched by moral and intellectual acceptance of the teaching of Christ as professed and lived in the Church. A people gathered together in this faith, proudly professing it, is fully open to and disposed for the grace of Baptism.

Because he is the custodian of the Church's faith and holiness the priest has the responsibility to ensure from his general pastoral care of his people and his particular preparation of those who are involved in each celebration of Baptism that these formulas of repentance and faith are truly meant.

Baptism

At the central moment of Baptism Christ is present and acting as truly as he is at the consecration of Mass. The reverence of the priest at this time will, more than anything else, convey the sacredness of the occasion.

It should be possible to arrange the parents, godparents and ministers around the font so that the congregation can have a view of what is happening; and the words spoken should be audible to all. In cold weather the water should be heated to a comfortable temperature. If the Baptism is not by immersion the water should be poured generously; it need not be poured in the form of a cross. It is sufficient for the godparents to stand close by; they do not have to touch the child during the actual Baptism.

Post-baptismal ceremonies

The immediate effects of Baptism are expressed in four symbolical rituals. The child is now a Christian, an anointed person. He has the baptismal character, by which he shares in the priestly, prophetic and kingly work of Christ, and can act as a member of his body, the Church. This is the meaning of *anointing with chrism*. A real, visible quantity of the oil should be applied, and it need not be wiped away immediately.

Dressing the child in a ceremonial *robe* expresses its new Christian dignity. The symbolism is more striking if there is a real putting on of a garment. Using something the child is already wearing, or a perfunctory laying of a cloth on its head does not mean much; and the stylised garments being produced commercially are less appropriate than an ordinary white baptismal shawl.

The taking of light from the paschal candle makes a link with the Easter mystery, source of the enlightenment the child has received in Baptism. When the father, or another representative of the family, lights the child's *candle* they are being reminded symbolically of the ability and obligation to pass on the light of Christ to their child.

Where it is done, the *Ephphetha* is a symbolical way of saying that the ears and mouth of the child have now been opened to hear and in due course speak the word of God.

While some of this symbolism may appear to be beyond an average congregation, the priest should not underestimate the power of symbolical actions even when they are not well understood, and the openness of parents to accept any sign of attention to and care for their child. The candle and robe can be retained as permanent reminders of the child's Baptism: the candle may, indeed, be used in family celebrations to mark the anniversary of Baptism or later stages in the child's sacramental life (e.g. First Communion).

e] Concluding rites *(Intro. 19)*

The transition to the final part of the ceremony can again be marked by a song and when possible by a procession to the altar. The altar is central to what is now done. The grace of Baptism will eventually lead the child to join its parents, friends and local church in the Eucharist. The saying of the Our Father at the altar — and the closer parents, godparents and the children can be arranged around the altar the better — is a symbolical anticipation of the fullness of Christian worship.

The final blessings and dismissal speak for themselves. They give the priest an opportunity to reach the hearts of his people, as he did when he received them at the beginning of the celebration, on a very human level, recognising the realities of their roles as mother, father, friends of a new-born child, and through his prayers and blessing giving them confidence to go out and fulfil their tasks.

Visit to shrine of our Lady

Where the custom of bringing the children to the shrine of our Lady immediately after their Baptism exists it "is observed if appropriate" *(Rite 71)*. Theological, liturgical and pastoral standards will be used to judge how appropriate the custom is in each particular place. Mary is the mother of believers, the first of the redeemed, the type and image of the Church. She is, therefore, appropriately venerated as the mother and model of those who are being reborn in Christ and initiated to the faith and life of the Church at Baptism. When this is the thinking behind the practice it will be seen to complement the sacrament and not compete with it.

The liturgical form of the devotion will be kept in proportion to the sacrament and the way it has been celebrated. It will be done after the blessing, perhaps while the final hymn (which could appropriately be the *Magnificat*) is being sung. If a prayer is said it should be brief; and since it is not part of the sacrament it might be said by one of the parents or by all together.

The effect of this devotion should be to deepen people's appreciation of Baptism. It will do this best if it reflects the self-effacing dignity of Mary at the great moments of her son's life. At Baptism, as at Cana (where he "manifested his glory; and his disciples believed in him") Mary's word still is "Do whatever he tells you" (*John 2:5-11*).

Bringing a baptised child to the church

A child who has been baptised without the full ritual of the sacrament is fully reborn in Christ and a member of the Church. But its status has yet to be recognised publicly in the Church. And those who will be responsible for its Christian formation — parents, godparents, local community and its priests — have yet to accept that responsibility in a public ecclesial act; and they have yet to surround the child with their welcome and their prayers. The rite for bringing a baptised child to the church provides the opportunity for thus completing the work of the sacrament. This is how its value and meaning should be explained to the faithful.

Although the elements of the rite are taken from the liturgy of the sacrament and are done in the same general way they have a different character. This is no "supplying of the ceremonies". The rite recognises that the child is already a Christian and treats him accordingly (e.g. *Rite 110*). The priest will need to reflect this difference in his manner of celebration. His homily, for example, will have a note of thanksgiving for what has been done, and will take account of the circumstances which led to the emergency Baptism. He will also be ready to adjust the words of the prayers accordingly (*Intro. 31,3; Rite,* 125).

Baptism during Mass

The manner of celebrating Baptism during Mass is described clearly in the *Introduction,* 29-30. The special value of celebrating the sacrament in this way lies in the connection it makes between Baptism and Eucharist. Baptism is initiation into the Christian life. The summit of that life is reached when the Christian community gathers, especially on Sundays, to celebrate the Eucharist and share in the Body of Christ. The baptised child will be educated in the faith and love of Christ so that one day it can take full part in this Eucharist and receive its first Holy Communion. On that day the Church will complete its welcome Meantime, parents, godparents and the local community will show their commitment to this task by offering the sacrifice of thanksgiving for the Baptism of their child, by praying for it and by themselves partaking in the Eucharist.

If parents do not wish to keep the newly baptised children in the church during the entire Mass they should arrange to have them taken away by others while they themselves remain for the full celebration. The priest will take advantage of the occasion to explain the significance of what is being done to his people, especially in the homily.

CEREMONY OF ADOPTION OF AN INFANT ALREADY BAPTISED

In the ceremony of adoption of an infant already baptised, the adoptive parents thank God for the gift of the adopted child, and commit themselves to rear the child in the Christian faith.

The ceremony may take place in church, or, if it seems preferable, in the home.

CHRISTIAN INITIATION OF ADULTS

Though infant Baptism is still the normal means of Christian initiation in Ireland, it should not be taken as the *norm* of Christian initiation. Baptism involves conversion from sin and faith in the Gospel of Christ. This is something that is achieved only gradually, only progressively, and is better expressed in adult Baptism.

The catechumenate, or time of preparation and probation for initiation, developed in the early Church as converts became numerous. It included not only instruction but also initiation into Christian worship, prayer and penance. It was a time when candidates were made aware of the implications of their Baptism and when their sincerity was tested. Emphasis was on formation rather than doctrinal instruction and candidates had to prove themselves before being admitted. Before they were finally admitted to Baptism at the Easter Vigil they presented themselves to the Church accompanied by members of the Christian community, who guaranteed their good intentions, and they were examined on the conduct of their lives during the period of preparation.

In the course of time, infant Baptism became normal practice; the catechumenate, which had been carried out in stages over a period of time, was shortened and telescoped into one ceremony, *The Rite for the Baptism of Adults,* the rite that we were familiar with. However, a decree of 1962 allowed once more the spreading out of the various stages of adult initiation, and then the Vatican Council's *Constitution on the Liturgy* decreed the restoration of the catechumenate: "The catechumenate for adults, comprising several distinct steps, is to be restored and brought into use at the discretion of the local Ordinary. By this means the time of the catechumenate, which is intended as a time of suitable instruction, may be sanctified by sacred rites to be celebrated at successive intervals of time" (*SC 64*). The Congregation for Divine Worship prepared a new rite for the Christian initiation of adults, the *Ordo of Baptism of Adults and Infants of Catechism Age,* which was promulgated on 6 January 1972. (Even if the catechumenate does not, at the moment, seem relevant to the situation in Ireland, there is much we can learn from it about Christian initiation and formation. It shows that Christian formation is not purely intellectual, that it does not consist merely in handing on ideas and precepts but is initiation into the life and mystery of Christ. It gives us a sense of the missionary character of the Church, that the Church is evangelical, and that all of us must take part in this work. It shows, above all, that growth in faith and conversion is the work of God, not of man.)

Rite of the Catechumenate received in stages

The *Introduction* to the new rite indicates that initiation takes place step by step in the midst of the community of the faithful. Baptism is initiation into the community of believers and the community has an important role to play in it. No one can become a catechumen all alone. He must experience, to some extent, the life of this community of faith. "Together with the catechumens, the faithful reflect upon the Paschal Mystery, renew their own conversion, and by their example lead the catechumens to obey the Holy Spirit more generously" (*4*). The spiritual journey of the catechumen is a time "for making inquiry and maturing". It is a time during which "the catechumen moves forward, as it were, through a gateway or up another step".

There are four main stages:
1. Evangelisation and precatechumenate
2. Catechumenate
3. Time of purification and enlightenment
4. Period of post-baptismal catechesis or mystagogy.

Then there are three rites by which one passes from one of

these stages to the next:
(a) Entrance to the catechumenate
(b) Inscription for Baptism
(c) Sacraments of initiation — Baptism, Confirmation, the Eucharist.

1 Evangelisation and precatechumenate

Strictly speaking, the rite of initiation begins with admission to the catechumenate, yet this period of evangelisation is of great importance and ordinarily should not be omitted. The new *Order* requires that the candidate be in possession of the elements of Christian doctrine and have undergone initial conversion before being admitted to the catechumenate. So the period of evangelisation is:
— a time when the Gospel is explained to inquirers.
— a time of search and questioning.
— a time to purify motives.
— a time to experience the spirit of the Christian life as it is lived within the community. The example and the support of the community is all important.
— a time when pastors should help inquirers with suitable prayers.
— a time, too, when the Church should befriend "sympathisers" — interested inquirers who "even if they do not fully believe, show an inclination toward the Christian faith".

Rite of becoming catechumens

This rite marks the transition from evangelisation to the catechumenate. It takes place when the candidates are prepared to declare publicly their desire to become Christians. It is desirable that the Christian community take an active part in the celebration. Sponsors should also be there to present the candidates, their friends, to the Church. One of the main features of the rite is the signing with the Sign of the Cross on the forehead and senses — a sign of Christ's love. "Christ will be your strength. Learn to know and follow him."

The rite consists of:

Reception of Candidates (assembled outside or at entrance).

Entry into the church.

Liturgy of the word, concluding with Intercessions for new catechumens.

Dismissal of catechumens (Eucharist may follow).

2 Catechumenate

The catechumenate or pastoral formation of catechumens presupposes initial faith and first conversion. It continues until the candidates have matured sufficiently in their conversion. This will vary from one individual to another, but may, if necessary, last for several years. It is not simply a time of catechetical or doctrinal instruction but a formation in Christian values and attitudes, and an introduction to the prayer-life and worship of the Christian community. " . . . the catechumens are well initiated into the mysteries of salvation, in the exercise of Gospel morality and in the sacred rites which are to be celebrated later on. In this way they are introduced into the life of faith, the liturgy and the charity of the people of God."

During this period instructions are given to the catechumens, showing them the whole Catholic teaching; their faith is enlightened, their hearts directed towards God, their participation in the liturgical mystery encouraged, their apostolic action aroused, their whole life nourished according to the spirit of Christ. *Celebrations of the Word of God*, adapted to the liturgical season, are held, serving both the instruction of the catechumens and the needs of the community. The *first or minor exorcisms* are performed in a prayerful and positive manner. These show the catechumens the true nature of the spiritual life as a battle between flesh and spirit, and underline both the importance of self-denial and the continuing need of

God's help. Blessings, which signify the love of God and the care of the Church, are offered to the catechumens so that while they still lack the grace of the sacraments, they may receive from the Church the spirit, joy and peace to continue their work and their spiritual journey. The catechumens think about finding godparents who will present them. The whole community should be assembled for some of the celebrations of the catechumenate and for the rites of transition. The community will have a part in the initiation of the catechumens.

In special cases, the local Ordinary, considering the spiritual preparation of the candidates, may shorten the period of the catechumenate. In singular cases he may allow it to take place in one celebration.

Rite of election or enrolment of names

This rite marks the transition from the catechumenate to the period of enlightenment and purification. The election or enrolment of names is celebrated at the beginning of Lent — the time of the proximate preparation for sacramental initiation. This is a decisive stage, when the candidates reaffirm their intention to proceed to the sacraments of initiation, and the Christian community, after deliberation and consultation, agrees to admit them. The Church hears the testimony of the godparents and catechists.

To be enrolled among the "elect" the candidates must have enlightened faith and have a deliberate intention of receiving the sacraments of the Church. The "elect" are admitted to the more intensive stage of preparation known as "Purification and Enlightenment". They are encouraged to advance toward Christ with even greater generosity.

The rite of election normally takes place on the First Sunday of Lent. It should take place within Mass after the homily. The order is as follows:

Presentation of the candidates by the one responsible for the catechumenate.

Questioning of the godparents about the suitability of candidates.

Examination of candidates.

Admission or election of candidates.

Prayer for the elect.

Dismissal of the elect.

3 Time of purification and enlightenment

This stage is marked by a more intense preparation of heart and spirit. It normally coincides with Lent, which in its liturgy and its liturgical catechesis, "is a memorial or a preparation for Baptism and a time of penance". Lent "renews the community of the faithful together with the catechumens and makes them ready to celebrate the paschal mystery which the sacraments of initiation apply to each individual".

During this time there is a more intense preparation of mind, which involves recollection more than catechesis. It is meant to purify minds and hearts by the examination of conscience and by repentance. It is also intended to give a deeper knowledge of Christ the Saviour. This is accomplished in various liturgical rites, particularly in the Scrutinies and Presentations.

Scrutinies

The Scrutinies have a two-fold purpose: (1) to reveal anything that is weak, defective or sinful in the hearts of the elect so that it may be healed, and (2) to reveal what is upright, strong and holy, so that it may be strengthened. This is achieved by exorcisms. The Scrutinies are intended to free them from sin and the devil and to give them strength in Christ. They are intended to make firm their decision.

There are three Scrutinies:

Prayer for the elect

Exorcism

Dismissal of the elect.

They are held, normally on the third, fourth and fifth

Sundays of Lent. They take place after the homily.

Presentations

These are rites by which the Church hands on to the elect its ancient documents of faith and prayer — the Profession of Faith or the Creed and the Lord's Prayer. It is desirable that these take place in the presence of the community of the faithful after the liturgy of the word at a weekday Mass.

a) Presentation of the Profession of Faith — this normally takes place during the week after the first Scrutiny. The elect are to memorise the Profession of Faith and then render it in public before they profess their faith in accordance with that creed on the day of their Baptism.

After the "tradition", there follow a Prayer for the Elect and a "laying on of hands" with a prayer.

b) Presentation of the Lord's Prayer — this normally takes place during the week after the third Scrutiny. From antiquity the Lord's Prayer belonged to those who had received the spirit of adoption of sons in Baptism.

After the "tradition" there is a Prayer for the Elect and a "laying on of hands" as above.

Preparatory rites

These rites are optional, but on Holy Saturday, when the "elect" refrain from work and spend their time in recollection, various preparatory rites may be celebrated: the recitation of the Creed, the *Ephphetha* or opening of the ears and mouth, the choosing of a Christian name, and even the anointing with oil of catechumens. Some or all of these may be used as desired:

Recitation of Profession of Faith — by which the elect are prepared to profess baptismal faith and are taught their duty of proclaiming the Gospel message.

Rite of Ephphetha — by its symbolism shows the need of grace for anyone to be able to hear the word of God and work for salvation.

Choosing of a Christian name — a new name may be given. It

must be a Christian name or one which in that part of the world has a Christian meaning.

Anointing with oil of catechumens — each elect is anointed on the breast or on both hands or even on other parts of the body.

Sacraments of initiation

The sacraments of Baptism, Confirmation and the Eucharist are the final stage in which the elect come forward and with their sins forgiven, are admitted into the people of God.

This normally takes place during the Easter Vigil, after the blessing of water, as indicated in the Order of the Easter Vigil (*No. 44*).

If it takes place outside the normal time, the celebration should be filled with the Easter spirit, using the ritual Mass from the missal.

The three sacraments are celebrated at the same time, thus restoring the ancient link between Baptism, Confirmation and the Eucharist as the sacraments of initiation.

If the bishop is not present the priest who baptises may confirm the candidates immediately after Baptism. This shows the close relationship between the mission of the Son and the pouring out of the Holy Spirit.

The first communion of the neophytes is the climax of their entire initiation and is the foundation of their Christian life. They are now members of a priestly people and so should take an active part in the Mass being celebrated — in the prayer of the faithful, in the preparation and procession of the gifts. Special mention is made of them in the eucharistic prayers. They may receive communion under both species.

4 Period of post-baptismal catechesis

This is the final stage of initiation. It normally coincides with Paschaltide. It is the time when the neophytes are helped by the community of the faithful, by their godparents and their pastors to enter more fully and joyfully into the life of the community.

The neophytes can achieve a fuller, more fruitful under-standing of the "mysteries" through this further catechesis, now that they have the new experience of receiving the sacraments and have a closer association with the Christian community.

The main place for post-baptismal catechesis is the Sunday Masses throughout the Easter season. The readings from Year A are appropriate.

At these Masses the neophytes should keep their special place among the faithful. They should take part in the Mass with their godparents. They should be mentioned in the homily and in the general intercessions.

To close the period of post-baptismal catechesis at the end of the Easter season, around Pentecost, some form of celebration is held.

On the anniversary of their Baptism it is desirable that the neophytes gather together again to give thanks to God, to share their spiritual experiences and gain new strength.

Simple rite of initiation

The simple rite of initiation given in the *Ordo of Christian Initiation of Adults*, 6 January 1972 may, with the permission of the bishop, be used on occasions, but it would be contrary to the mind of the Church to use it habitually. It may be used:

1. when the candidate cannot go through all the stages of initiation, or
2. when the local Ordinary, judging that the candidate is sincere in his conversion to Christianity and in his religious maturity, permits him to receive Baptism without delay.

This rite may be carried out in *one* celebration, or one or two of the rites from the catechumenate or from the period of purification may be celebrated before the celebration of the sacraments.

Before he is baptised, the candidate should choose a godparent and spend some time with the local community. He should be instructed and prepared for a suitable period of time to purify his motives for seeking Baptism, so that he may become more mature in his conversion and his faith.

As far as possible, the celebration takes place on a Sunday with active participation of the local community.

The rite normally takes place during Mass.

After Baptism and Confirmation the neophyte takes part in the Eucharist for the first time.

Short rite of initiation in danger of death

This rite is given in the *Ordo of Christian Initiation of Adults,* 6 January, 1972. It is especially suitable for use by catechists and by lay people.

If those baptised in danger of death should recover their health, they are given suitable formation, received at the church at a fitting time, and then are given the rest of the sacraments of initiation.

Preparing uncatechised adults for Confirmation and the Eucharist

This rite is given in the *Ordo of Christian Initiation of Adults*, 6 January, 1972. It is for those adults baptised as infants but who did not receive further catechetical formation and did not receive Confirmation and the Eucharist.

The catechumenate is adapted to meet this situation.

The conversion of such adults is based on the Baptism they have already received, and they must unfold its power.

Their catechetical formation should correspond to the one suggested for catechumens. Their Christian life should be strengthened by suitable discipline and the teaching given to them, by contact with the community of believers and by taking part in certain liturgical rites.

RITE OF INITIATION FOR CHILDREN OF CATECHETICAL AGE

This rite is for children, unbaptised as infants, who have reached the age of reason and are able to be taught. They have either been brought by their parents or have come of their own accord with parental permission. For these a simplified form of the catechumenate is provided, adapted to their understanding. The rite is given in the *Ordo of Christian Initiation of Adults and Infants of Catechism Age*, 6 January, 1972.

The families of these children have an important role to play, as has also the catechetical community of which the children are members.

During the celebration the children go to their parents and ask their consent to be made Christians.

RITE OF RECEPTION OF BAPTISED CHRISTIANS INTO FULL COMMUNION WITH THE CATHOLIC CHURCH

In an appendix to the *Ordo of Christian initiation of Adults*, January 6, 1972, there is a rite for receiving into the Catholic Church those born and baptised in a separated ecclesial communion.

The whole approach in this rite is ecumenical, and the rite is so arranged that no greater burden than is necessary is demanded for reception.

The baptised Christian should, normally, receive both doctrinal and spiritual preparation for his reception into full communion with the Catholic Church.

For Eastern Christians nothing more than a simple profession of faith is required.

Anything that has the appearance of triumphalism should be carefully avoided.

Confusion between catechumens and candidates for reception into communion should be absolutely avoided.

No abjuration of heresy is required of one born and baptised outside the visible communion of the Catholic Church, but a profession of faith.

The sacrament of Baptism is not to be celebrated as a matter of course. Conditional Baptism is not permitted unless there is a reasonable doubt about the fact or validity of Baptism already received.

Episcopal Conferences may adapt the foregoing rites to suit the conditions and circumstances of persons and places. The celebrant, too, should use fully and intelligently the freedom which is given to him either in the *General Introduction* or in the rubrics of the rite.

The community must always be ready to carry out its apostolic vocation by giving help to those who need Christ. They should, as far as possible, be present at the important celebrations of initiation.

2 Confirmation

Confirmation, the gift of the Spirit

Those who have been baptised continue on the path of Christian initiation through the sacrament of Confirmation. In this sacrament they receive the Holy Spirit, who was sent upon the apostles by the Lord at Pentecost.

The Spirit in the life of Jesus
The Spirit was present in Jesus the Son of God from the beginning. Mary conceived him by the power of the Holy Spirit. At his Baptism in the Jordan the Spirit descended upon him (*Mk 1:10*) establishing him as messianic witness of the Father (*Acts 10:38*) and as the one who would baptise others with the Holy Spirit (*Jn 1:33*). Through the power of the Spirit Jesus preached, worked miracles, prayed and died (*Heb 9:14*). This Jesus who died for us was raised from the dead by the Father and established as universal Lord and Saviour through the Spirit (*Eph 1:17ff; Rom 1:4*).

The risen Jesus shares his Spirit with us
The risen Lord now communicates this same Holy Spirit to his Church so that we are his Body sharing in the very life of the Trinity itself. The Spirit of the risen Christ completes our redemption. "Through Christ, the Word made flesh, man has access to the Father in the Holy Spirit and comes to share in the

divine nature" (*Eph 2:18; 2 Pet 1:4*) (cf. *DV 1,2*).

The Spirit in Christian living

The Holy Spirit is at work in our lives now as he was at work in the life of Christ. Just as the whole ministry of Jesus was sustained and perfected by the Spirit, the whole of Christian living and of the life of the Church today is sustained by the Spirit. This one Spirit of the risen Christ is the Spirit of resurrection and hope, giving us the strength to face the responsibilities and disappointments of life. The Spirit offers us forgiveness in our own failings and unkept promises, and gives us the courage to experience and share the peace of Christ our brother.

The Spirit prays with us, and on our journey through life we are led by the Spirit of Truth who calls us to hold high the light of the Gospel before the world. What seems at times impossible from the human point of view becomes possible through the power of the Spirit.

Sacraments of initiation

In Christian living we are incorporated into the mystery of Christ through the Church and sacraments. But where we encounter Christ we also encounter his Spirit. We encounter the Spirit, therefore, through the Church's sacraments. And this is particularly so in the case of the three sacraments by which we become Christians: Baptism into Christ, Confirmation in the Spirit, and the Eucharist, which builds up the Church in the unity of Christ through the power of the Spirit.

In Baptism we are incorporated into God's family, sharing in the Spirit of Christ's sonship. "By one Spirit we were all baptised into one body" (*1 Cor 12:13*). At Confirmation our Baptism is completed or "sealed" by the gift of the Spirit of Pentecost. In the Eucharist we are fed by the bread of life which nourishes the family of God through the power of the Spirit.

The Confirmation of Baptism

Baptism into Christ is always Baptism in the Spirit. However, if the Spirit is received already in Baptism, how then, is Confirmation different from this sacrament? Answers to this question will always remain unconvincing if they are given solely in terms of the "essential differences" between these two sacraments, instead of in terms of their close relationship to each other.

Gift of Pentecost

The language of the New Testament indicates that Baptism is always associated with new life as participation in the death and resurrection of Christ (*Rom 6:3*f.; *Col 2:11*f.). However, the New Testament also speaks of the messianic "gift of the Spirit" (*Jn 7:37*f.) which is given to Christians as the foundation of their calling or mission to witness and announce the Christian message to the world. "You will receive power when the Holy Spirit comes on you, and then you will be my witnesses not only in Jerusalem but throughout Judea and Samaria, and indeed to the ends of the earth" (*Acts 1:8*).

At Pentecost the Church received this "gift of the Spirit" from the glorified Christ established in power (cf. *Acts 2:33*). The ministry of Jesus was perfected only when he was established in power by the Father as the sender of the Spirit of Pentecost. So too, our incorporation into the death and resurrection of Jesus at Baptism is completed through the "gift of the Spirit" given to us at Confirmation. It is for this reason, also, that in the early Church, Baptism is linked with the mystery of Christ's death and resurrection, and Confirmation is linked with the mystery of Pentecost.

Calling to witness

Every Christian is called to share in the prophetic mission of Christ. Through Confirmation, the sacrament of the pentecostal "gift of the Spirit", we are called to be Christ's witnesses before the world. "Bound more intimately to the

Church by the sacrament of Confirmation, they (Christians) are endowed by the Holy Spirit with special strength. Hence they are more strictly obliged to spread and defend the faith both by word and by deed as true witnesses of Christ" (*LG 2, 11*).

Calling to service

The "gift of the Spirit" received at Confirmation must be effective in a practical way within the Christian community. It is for this reason that the Spirit of Pentecost manifests himself through charisms, that is, through special gifts given to every Christian to be used in the service of the community. "Each has his own special gift from God, one of one kind, and one of another" (*1 Cor 7:7*). "To each is given the manifestation of the Spirit for the common good" (*1 Cor 12:7*). In Confirmation the Church recognises that every Christian has a unique calling or vocation in the Spirit. Through the gifts or talents assigned to them, every Christian has a contribution to make in society.

Confirmation, then, is the sacrament of the Holy Spirit which says to young Christians: "Let everyone lead the life which the Lord has assigned to him, and in which God has called him" in the Spirit (*1 Cor 7:17*).

Preparation

Role of parents, teachers and priests

Even though the children preparing for Confirmation are instructed in school, nevertheless parents and priests also should be involved in this work of preparation.

The priests of the parish should visit the schools during the months before Confirmation, and make themselves familiar with the rite of Confirmation and with the catechetical programme of the Confirmation class.

The rite of Confirmation emphasises the obligation of parents to ensure that their children are adequately prepared. For this reason meetings between parents, teachers and priests should be arranged. At least two such meetings should be held.

These would deal with:

The role of the Holy Spirit in the Church and in the lives of individual Christians.

The effects of Confirmation as outlined above.

The responsibilities of parents in the religious education of their children. In this connection parents can help children to prepare for the coming of the Holy Spirit at Confirmation by encouraging responsible attitudes, and above all by the parents' own example of prayer and Christian living.

An explanation of the rite of Confirmation itself, together with a discussion of practical details such as time of ceremony, sponsors, names, "pledge", etc.

Excellent filmstrips are available on these matters.

Shortly before Confirmation the priests should arrange a service of preparation, e.g., Mass, prayer service, or a short retreat, in which children, parents, teachers and priests all take part.

Sponsors

The sponsor's role is to bring the candidate to receive the sacrament, present him to the bishop for anointing, and help him, later, to fulfil his baptismal promises faithfully under the influence of the Holy Spirit.

It is desirable that the sponsor at Baptism also be the sponsor at Confirmation. A special sponsor may be chosen, and even the parents themselves may act as sponsors for their children. The sponsor should be a Catholic and sufficiently mature for his role.

Rehearsal and music preparation

A detailed rehearsal for the ceremony of Confirmation is recommended. This will help to ensure a dignified celebration, and to acquaint the congregation with the music programme selected for the ceremony.

Although the communal nature of the celebration is underlined by well prepared and well coordinated singing of the whole assembly, a meditative atmosphere appropriate to the occasion could be created by some choral singing during the administration of the sacrament, or during other carefully selected moments.

When the sacrament is to be administered to children of several schools, the music programme should be agreed upon well in advance, and adequate preparation time given.

Announcement of Confirmation to parishioners

Confirmation is a community celebration, and should be well publicised beforehand. The date and time should be announced well in advance, and the significance of the sacrament explained to the people.

Before the ceremony

1. Provide Confirmation cards for all candidates.[1]
2. Have a typewritten list of all candidates' names.
3. Arrange for appointment of sponsors.
4. Choose children, as many as possible, for the various activities such as acting as cantors, proclaiming the readings, reciting the intentions at the Prayer of the Faithful, bringing the gifts to the altar, etc.
5. Arrange rehearsal and music preparation as indicated above.

Immediate preparation

1. Text of Mass. The ritual Mass of Confirmation, given in the Missal, may be used on any day except the Sundays of Advent, Lent and Easter; solemnities, Ash Wednesday and the weekdays of Holy Week.
2. Vestments. Red or white are worn.
3. Servers. Eight required: thurifer, incense-bearer, cross-bearer, two servers to carry candles, server to hold book for bishop, mitre and crozier bearers.

---

[1] Confirmation cards should give a) surname, b) Christian name, c) Confirmation name if used, d) address, e) names of parents, f) date of Baptism, g) place of Baptism, h) place of Confirmation, i) date of Confirmation, j) Minister of Confirmation.

4. Breadcrumbs or cotton wool, a sliced lemon, warm water, soap and towel for removing chrism from bishop's hands.

Note: It is no longer required to remove chrism from candidate's forehead after anointing.

5. Mitre, crozier and sacred chrism are provided by bishop.

After the ceremony

The names of those confirmed, their parents, the sponsors and the bishop and the date and place of Confirmation should be recorded in a special book, in addition to the entries in the baptismal register.

Where children are baptised outside their parish, notification should be sent to their place of baptism.

Confirmation of adults

The Confirmation of adults may take place, if so desired, on the occasion of Confirmation in the parish. Adults who are being presented for Confirmation should be given an appropriate catechetical preparation. When presented for Confirmation they should have a Confirmation card as indicated above for children's Confirmation.

The liturgy of Confirmation

Ordinarily Confirmation takes place within Mass.

Role of bishop

In the person of the bishops, the Lord Jesus Christ, supreme High Priest, is present in the midst of the faithful (*LG 21*). The bishops, as successors of the apostles, usually administer the sacrament of Confirmation. When the apostles, Peter and John, heard that the people of Samaria had received the gift of Baptism, they went to give them the Holy Spirit (cf. *Acts* 8:14-17). In the same way, the bishops go to the children of the parish community when they are ready to receive the sacrament of Confirmation.

Entrance procession

While the entrance antiphon is being sung the bishop, ministers, and, if desired, those to be confirmed, enter in procession and take their places. It is desirable that the procession be led by a thurifer followed by cross-bearer and servers with lighted candles.

Liturgy of the word

The readings may be taken in whole or in part either from the texts in the lectionary for Confirmation, or from the Mass of the day.

Presentation of candidates

Children should be called individually except where large numbers make this difficult. When the name is called the child stands and, at the appropriate time, approaches the bishop, accompanied by the sponsor.

Renewal of baptismal promises

Here the children make for themselves the promises that were made on their behalf at Baptism. The renewal of the baptismal promises takes the place of the Creed.

The laying on of hands

The laying on of hands is an ancient biblical form of calling on God asking him to give his blessing to someone (cf. *Gen 48:14*). Jesus himself imposes hands, e.g. in the blessing of children (*Mk 10:16*) and in curing people (cf. *Mk 6:5, 8:23-25: Lk 4:40, 13:13*). The apostles and the early Church follow Jesus's example. They also impose hands as a sign that someone is being given a special task in the community (cf. *Acts 6:1-6*). Imposition of hands is used particularly to indicate that someone is being given the "gift of the Spirit": after praying for the people of Samaria, Peter and John imposed hands on them and "they received the Holy Spirit" (cf. *Acts 8:14*f.).

Anointing with chrism

The sacrament of Confirmation is conferred by the anointing with chrism on the forehead, which is done by the imposition of the hand, and by the words of the accompanying formula.

The bishop sits, wearing the mitre, and with gremial veil or amice on his knees. The candidate kneels before the bishop. An assisting priest takes the candidate's Confirmation card, and gives the Christian name (and Confirmation name if used) to the bishop. (Though no longer necessary, a Confirmation name may still be taken.) The sponsor places his or her right hand on the shoulder of the candidate. An assisting priest ensures that the forehead can be easily anointed.

In the Old Testament kings and priests were anointed with oil to show that they were called by God to a special mission, and to give them God's spirit to strengthen them in that mission. In the sacrament of Confirmation the bishop anoints the candidate with chrism, which is a mixture of olive oil and balsam. Thus the candidate is filled with the Holy Spirit, who will be with him through his life to strengthen him in his mission as a member of the Church and a witness of Christ in the world. The sweet fragrance of the balsam recalls to mind St Paul's reference to the good odour of Christ whose presence the Christian will spread among men.

The child answers "Amen" to the formula of anointing. It is an "Amen" both of faith and of gratitude: through it the child expresses his faith, and his gratitude for the gift of the Holy Spirit. The child answers "And also with you" to the bishop's "Peace be with you". Child and sponsor then return to their places.

It may be helpful to introduce singing into the celebration during the anointing, once the formula has been heard by the people.

Final blessing and dismissal

A special solemn form of the blessing is used. After each invocation the congregation answers "Amen".

Note: Children who have been previously confirmed in danger of death should be admitted to the Confirmation class and should take part in the ceremony. They should not, of course, be admitted to sacramental anointing. To save disappointment and embarrassment such children might be brought to the officiating bishop for a special blessing.

3 The Eucharist

THE CELEBRATION OF THE EUCHARIST

The Mass is the centre of the whole Christian life. It is the culminating act by which God in Christ sanctifies the world, and men through Christ adore the Father.

At the Last Supper Christ instituted the Mass, the eucharistic sacrifice of his body and blood, to perpetuate the sacrifice of the cross throughout the centuries until he comes again. He entrusted it to the Church as a memorial of his death and resurrection.

The Lord's Supper or Mass gathers together the people of God, with a priest presiding in the person of Christ, to celebrate this memorial of the Lord, or eucharistic sacrifice. It is the Church's great act of praise and thanksgiving, a sacrament of love, a sign of unity, a bond of charity, a paschal banquet in which Christ is consumed, the mind is filled with grace, and a pledge of future glory is given to us (cf. *SC 47*, *IG 1,2,7*).

The presiding celebrant

Bishop
Every authentic celebration of the Eucharist is directed by the bishop, either in person or through priests, his helpers (*IG 59*). Whenever he is present at a Mass with a congregation the bishop should preside over the assembly, and associate the priests with himself in the celebration. Among the forms of eucharistic celebration in the local church this form, with the

48

bishop presiding over his priest and people, is the most important; in this way the Church is most clearly manifested (*IG 74*). If he does not celebrate the Eucharist but assigns another to celebrate, the bishop may properly preside during the liturgy of the word and may conclude the Mass with the dismissal rite (*IG 59*). On such occasions he should keep in mind that by receiving Communion he takes part more perfectly in the celebration of the Eucharist (*EM 31*).

Priest

The priest too possesses the power of orders to offer the sacrifice of the Eucharist in the person of Christ (cf. *IG 60*). It is he alone who consecrates the bread and wine, although all the faithful constitute a holy people which plays its own role in the Eucharist (cf. *EM 12*). The distinctive nature of the ministerial priesthood is clear from the prominent place the priest occupies, and the functions he takes in the rite itself: offering sacrifice in the person of Christ and presiding over the assembly of God's holy people (*IG 4*). In doing this he joins the offering of the faithful to the sacrifice of Christ, re-presenting and applying in the sacrifice of the Eucharist the one sacrifice of the New Testament (*LG 28*). It is in the mystery of the eucharistic sacrifice that the priest fulfils his chief duty, sharing in the mediatory role of Christ (*PO 13; LG 28*). In the celebration of the Eucharist the priest openly acknowledges that he celebrates in union with the bishop (*PO 7*).

Function of the presiding celebrant

It is the function of the presiding celebrant to:
preside over the assembled faithful;
lead them in prayer;
proclaim the message of salvation;
lead the faithful in offering the sacrifice through Christ in the Spirit to the Father;
give the faithful the bread of eternal life, and share it with them (*IG 60*).

In exercising his function at the Eucharist, the priest should do only what belongs to him, so that in the liturgy the Church may be seen in its variety of orders and ministeries (*IG 2,58*). He should allow the faithful to take their own part, carrying out their own particular functions of reading, singing, announcing the intentions of the general intercessions, etc. (*IG 63-71*).

Attitudes of celebrant

At the Eucharist the priest should serve God and the faithful with dignity and humility. By his actions and by his proclamations of the word, he should impress upon the faithful the living presence of Christ (*IG 60*). He should not be content with the exact fulfilment of his role according to the liturgical laws (*EM 20*) but should, by the very way in which he celebrates the liturgy, convey an awareness of the meaning of the sacred rites. He should preside in such a way that the faithful will know that they are attending not a rite established on private initiative, but the Church's public worship (*EM 45*). The priest should remember that the effectiveness of the liturgy does not consist in the continual search for newer rites or simpler forms, but in an ever deeper insight into the word of God and the mystery being celebrated. The priest who imposes his own personal reforms of sacred rites offends the rights of the faithful and introduces individualism and idiosyncrasy into celebrations which belong to the whole Church (*L1*).

Presidential prayers

Among the parts assigned to the priest, the eucharistic prayer has precedence; it is the high point of the whole celebration, the great thanksgiving prayer during which the faithful join with Christ in praising the works of God and offering sacrifice. In proclaiming this prayer the priest expresses the voice of God as it is addressed to the people, and the voice of the people as they turn to God. He alone should proclaim it, while the faithful observe a reverent silence (*IG 10; EP 8*). The final doxology, "through him, with him, etc.", is part of the eucharistic prayer.

It is not an acclamation of the people, and should not be said by them, but by the priest alone.

Next are the prayers: the opening prayer or collect, the prayer over the gifts, and the prayer after communion. These, with the eucharistic prayer, are called "presidential prayers" because the priest, presiding in the person of Christ, addresses them to God in the name of the entire assembly of God's people and of all present (*IG 10*). The nature of the presidential prayers demands that they be spoken in a loud and clear voice so that everyone present may hear and pay attention. While the priest is speaking, there should be no other prayer or song, and the organ and other musical instruments should be silent (*IG 12*). When the priest says a prayer, especially a eucharistic prayer, he should avoid both a dry monotonous style of delivery, and an overly subjective and emotional way of speaking and acting (*EP 17*). His style of speech should be suited to the nature of the particular text according as it is a reading, a prayer, a directive, etc.; it should take into account also the form of the celebration and its degree of solemnity (*IG 18*).

Other prayers and words of the presiding celebrant

As president of the congregation the priest also gives instructions and words of introduction and conclusion indicated in the rites; he proclaims the word of God and gives the final blessing.

He may also say a few words at certain moments throughout the celebration to draw the people into fuller understanding of and participation in the Eucharist. These few words or *monitiones* may be spoken before the celebration begins, before the readings, before the preface, and before the dismissal. There are other *monitiones* given in the missal which need not be used in the exact form in which they appear, but which may be adapted to the varying circumstances of the congregation. Examples are those given for the penitential rite and before the Our Father. In no case should these *monitiones* become a sermon or homily. Care should be taken to keep them brief and not too wordy, for otherwise they become tedious (*EP 14*). Moreover, they should be carefully prepared (*IG 68*).

Priest's use of song

The hierarchical and community nature of the liturgy (*MS 5*) is shown forth when the president sings the parts allocated to him, and the people respond in song. Of particular importance are:

the dialogue before the preface, and the preface;
the invitatory "Let us proclaim the mystery of faith";
the doxology "Through him, with him," etc.

A priest who cannot sing should render these texts in a loud and distinct voice (*MS 8*). Singing is, after all, a stylised form of proclamation.

Effective use of music can be made also at the greeting and dismissal. As a mark of honour to the Gospel, the chants preceding and following it may be sung.

"It is desirable that the priest should join his voice to the voice of the whole faithful in those words which concern the people" (*MS 26*).

Prayers said "Secreto"

As president the priest prays in the name of the whole community. At times too he prays in his own name so that he may exercise his ministry with attention and devotion. These prayers are said *secreto*, i.e. inaudibly (*IG 13*).

Silence

A sacred silence should be observed at certain times in order that the texts may achieve their full effect and enable the greatest possible spiritual benefits to be gained. As an integral part of the liturgy, silence allows people to become recollected or to meditate briefly on what they have heard, or to pray and praise God in their hearts (*EP 18*).

The worshipping community

The ministerial priesthood throws light on another and important priesthood, namely, the royal priesthood of believers. Their spiritual sacrifice to God is accomplished through the ministry of priests, in union with the sacrifice of Christ, our one and only mediator. The celebration of the Eucharist is the action of the whole Church, in which each individual should take his own full part and only his part, as determined by his particular position in the people of God. In this way greater attention is given to some aspects of the eucharistic celebration which have sometimes been overlooked in the course of time. The worshipping community is the people of God, won by Christ with his blood, called together by the Lord, and nourished by his word. It is a people called to offer God the prayers of the entire human family, a people which gives thanks in Christ for the mystery of salvation by offering his sacrifice. It is a people brought together and strengthened in unity by sharing in the body and blood of Christ. This people is holy in origin, but by conscious, active, and fruitful participation in the mystery of the Eucharist it constantly grows in holiness (*IG 5*).

Preparation

Catechesis
Suitable catechesis is essential if the mystery of the Eucharist is to take deeper root in the minds and lives of the faithful (*EM 5*). Such catechesis should aim at helping the faithful to realise that the celebration of the Eucharist is the true centre of the whole Christian life (*EM 6*).

Catechesis of the Eucharist should take account of the following:
1. The Mass, the Supper of the Lord, is at the same time and inseparably:
a sacrifice, in which the sacrifice of the cross is perpetuated;

a memorial of the death and resurrection of the Lord;
a sacred banquet in which through the communion of the body
and blood of the Lord the people of God share the benefits of
the paschal sacrifice, renew the new covenant which God has
made with man once for all through the blood of Christ, and in
faith and hope foreshadow and anticipate the eschatological
banquet in the kingdom of the Father, proclaiming the Lord's
death "till his coming" (*EM 3a*).

2. In the Mass the sacrifice and sacred banquet belong to the
same mystery, so much so that they are linked by the closest
bond. Participation in the sacred banquet is always communion
with Christ offering himself for us as a sacrifice to the Father.

3. The celebration of the Eucharist is the action not only of
Christ but also of his Church. The Church, the spouse and
minister of Christ, performs together with him the role of priest
and victim, offering him to the Father, and at the same time
offering herself together with him. The term "victim" as
applied to Christ is unique, but he unites the offering of his
Church to the offering of himself.

4. Hence no Mass is a purely private act, but rather a
celebration of the whole Church.

5. The celebration of the Eucharist is the origin and purpose of
the worship shown to the Eucharist outside Mass (*EM 3*).

6. The celebration of the Eucharist is the true centre of the
whole Christian life. It is the summit of both the action by
which God sanctifies the world in Christ, and the worship
which men offer to the Father through Christ in the Spirit
(*EM 6*).

7. Where the faithful gather for the Eucharist, there the
Church of Christ is truly present (*EM 7*).

8. The Eucharist is the sign of unity of believers, and it effects
that unity.

9. The principal ways in which our Lord is present in the
Eucharist are: a) in the faithful; b) in the word; c) in the person
of the celebrant; d) above all, *speciali modo*, in the sacred species
(*EM 9*).

10. The liturgy of the word and the liturgy of the Eucharist constitute a single act of worship. The wonders which the word proclaims culminate in the Paschal Mystery, of which the memorial is celebrated sacramentally in the Eucharist (*EM 10*).

11. Through the re-birth of Baptism and the anointing of the Spirit the faithful are consecrated into a holy priesthood. Their priesthood differs, however, from that of the ministerial priesthood not merely in degree but in essence (*EM 11*).

12. The role of the faithful in the Eucharist is:

to listen to the word, and respond to it;

to recall the passion, resurrection and glorification of the Lord;

to give thanks to God;

to offer the immaculate victim not only through the hands of the priest but together with him;

to offer themselves to God, as members of the Mystical Body, in union with Christ, their Head;

finally, by receiving the body of the Lord, to perfect that union with God and among themselves which should be the product of participation in the sacrifice (*EM 12*).

The Church has stressed repeatedly (*EM passim; EP 17,19*) the need to instruct the faithful on the Eucharist. Such instruction, rather than the introduction of novelties, will help the faithful to understand the Eucharist better, and take part in it more fully (*EP 19*). In particular, the faithful should be instructed on the nature and purpose of the eucharistic prayer (*EP 5*). A basis for such instruction will be found below, page 67.

Arranging the celebration

It is of the greatest importance that the celebration of the Eucharist be so arranged that the ministers and faithful may take their own proper part in it, and thus gain its fruits more fully (*IG 2*). In particular, the nature and circumstances of the particular assembly should be considered (*IG 3*). All concerned should work together in preparing the celebration, under the direction of the priest in charge (*IG 73*).

Where there are large congregations, someone should be designated to arrange the celebration and see that the ceremonies are carried out in a devout and orderly manner (*IG 69*). The pastoral effectiveness of the celebration depends in great measure on the choice of readings, prayers and chants which correspond to the needs, spiritual preparation and attitude of the faithful. In planning the celebration priests should consider the spiritual good of the faithful rather than their own desires. The choice of texts is to be made in consultation with ministers and others who have a function in the celebration (*IG 313*).

Liturgy preparation team

A liturgy preparation team can play an important role in the planning of the liturgy. The team should consist of those who have a particular function in the celebration (reader, cantor, sacristan, person in charge of altar servers, collectors, organist, choir master, etc.) together with representatives of the community. The team makes the practical preparation for the liturgy under the guidance of the priest.

"Since so many choices are now possible, it is necessary to make sure that the deacon, lector, psalmist, cantor, commentator and choir should all know beforehand what they have to do" (*IG 313*).

All involved in the preparation of the liturgy should receive "suitable liturgical and spiritual formation" (*MS 24*) so that in their service to the whole community they may be deeply penetrated with the spirit of the liturgy (*SC 29*).

The celebration of the Eucharist

In the celebration of the Eucharist the faithful form a holy people, a chosen race, a royal priesthood, united through and with Christ in the worship of the Father. They should make this clear by their deep sense of religion and their charity to everyone (*IG 62*). Accordingly in the celebration of the

Eucharist a sense of community should be encouraged; each person will then feel himself united with his brethren in the communion of the Church, local and universal, and even with all men (*EM 18*). Any appearance of individualism or division among the faithful should be avoided, since they are brothers in the sight of the one Father. They should become one body, hearing the word, joining in prayers and hymns, and offering sacrifice and sharing the Lord's table together (*IG 62*).

Diversity of roles

Everyone in the eucharistic assembly has the right and duty to take his own part according to the diversity of orders and functions (*IG 58*). By taking their own particular part, whether through reading, singing, announcing the intentions during the prayers of the faithful, etc., the faithful will gain the fruits of the sacrifice more fully (*IG 2, 66*).

Vocal participation of the faithful

Because the Eucharist is a communal action, the dialogue between celebrant and congregation, and the acclamations are of special value. These are not only external signs of the communal celebration, but are also the means of greater communication between celebrant and people (*IG 14*).

Song

Singing should be used widely in the eucharistic celebration. Preference should be given to the more significant parts, especially those to be sung by the celebrant or ministers, with the faithful responding, or those to be sung by celebrant and faithful together. The faithful should know how to sing some parts at least of the Ordinary in Latin, expecially the Creed and Our Father (*IG 19*).

[Pope Paul VI has frequently expressed the desire that all the faithful should know at least some Latin Gregorian chants, such as, for example, the Gloria, the Credo, the Sanctus and the Agnus Dei. (See letter of *Sacred Congregation for Divine Worship*, April 1974). These, together with some of the better known and easy Gregorian melodies suitable for congregational singing are to be found in *Jubilate Deo*, CTS, London. On the question of language, the *Constitution on the Liturgy* says that the use of the Latin language is to be preserved in the Latin rites, with due respect to particular law (*No. 36*).]

Deciding what parts of Mass are to be sung

A celebration which uses music effectively is not necessarily one in which every singable text is sung. In fact the structure of the Mass emerges more clearly in a celebration where a judicious choice of sung parts is made. The *General Instruction on the Roman Missal* does not attempt to set forth a definitive and complete set of priorities. It does, however, give certain guiding principles:

1. The more important parts of the Mass should be sung (*IG 19*).
2. The purpose of the singing will determine the kind of singing, e.g. acclamation, dialogue, meditation.
3. The capabilities and dispositions of the community should be considered (*IG 19*).

Preference should be given normally to:

1. The acclamations: Gospel acclamation; Sanctus; Memorial acclamation; Great Amen.
2. The responsorial psalm.

The varied roles which singing plays at these and other moments throughout the Mass are discussed at the relevant points of the text, below.

The choir

The choir is a section of the assembled community and has a special task (*IG 274*):

a. to sing the parts allocated to it;
b. to encourage the active participation of the people.

At certain moments the choir may sing alone. These include:

1. the Preparation of the Gifts;
2. Communion;
3. after the dismissal.

(The singing by the choir of a *Kyrie, Gloria, Credo* and *Agnus Dei* from the Gregorian or polyphonic repertoire can, on occasion, be effective.)

On these occasions the people participate internally (*MS 15a*) by listening to the music of the choir, which can "raise their hearts to God" (cf. *MS 5*).

At other moments the choir may alternate with the people. These moments include the *Kyrie, Gloria, Credo* and *Agnus Dei*.

At other moments the choir may sing with the people, reinforcing their singing by the addition of harmonies and musical elaboration. This can be particularly effective at the acclamations.

The success of the choir depends to a great extent on its location. It should be located in such a place that it can easily carry out its functions (*IG 274*) and be seen as part of the Christian assembly.

Cantor

The cantor's main role is to sing the Responsorial Psalm. However, in places where there is no choir, or at celebrations which the choir cannot attend, he may lead the congregational singing (*MS 21*). A leader of congregational singing can do much to help and encourage the people even when a choir is present. It is important that the cantor be trained not only in musical matters, but also in correct and articulate pronounciation (*IG 67*).

When he acts in the capacity of "psalmist", that is when he sings the Responsorial Psalm, he should stand at the ambo. When giving directions to the people, and in leading them in song he should not stand at the ambo — which should be reserved for the Word of God — but in some other suitable place where he can be seen by the people (*IG 68a*).

The reader

Traditionally, the reading of the scriptures is considered a ministerial, not a presidential, function. It is desirable that the gospel be read by a deacon or, in his absence, by a priest other than the one presiding; the other readings are proclaimed by a reader (*IG 34*). The reader, although a layman, has his own proper function in the eucharistic celebration, and should exercise this even though ministers of a higher rank are present. By "reader" the *IG* seems to refer to a person officially commissioned to this ministry. Since the reading is to develop in the faithful a profound appreciation of scripture, the reader should be competent and carefully prepared (cf. *IG 66*). In addition to his technical vocal competence in communication, the reader must have a deep appreciation of the sacredness of the office he is carrying out. Through the words which the reader pronounces Christ himself speaks to the faithful (*SC 7*).

Place of celebration

Normally the Eucharist should be celebrated in a church, or if there is none, some other worthy place (*IG 253*). Priests should realise that the way in which the church is arranged greatly contributes to a worthy celebration, and to the active participation of the people (*EM 24*). Temporary arrangements made in recent years should gradually be given a final form. Some of these temporary solutions although reproved are still in use, though they are liturgically and artistically unsatisfactory, and render difficult the worthy celebration of the Eucharist (*LI 10*). The buildings and requisites for worship, as signs and symbols of heavenly things, should be truly worthy and beautiful (*IG 253*).

The rite of Mass

Introductory rites, from entrance of priest to opening prayer, inclusive.
Purpose: To make the assembled people a unified community

and to prepare them to listen to God's word and celebrate the Eucharist (*IG 25*).

Entrance of priests and ministers
Entrance procession: Thurible, cross, candles, gospel book may be carried (*IG 82*).

Entrance song
Purpose: To open the celebration; deepen the unity of the people; introduce them to the mystery of the season or feast; and accompany the procession (*IG 25*). If there is no song the antiphon is recited by the people or reader; otherwise, by the celebrant himself after the greeting (*IG 26*).

The nature and purpose of the entrance song show that congregational participation in it is highly desirable. Music as the bond of unity makes the gathered community more aware of its identity as the people of God, called together in one place to hear his word and to celebrate the Eucharist. The entrance song adds an element of solemnity to the entrance procession which it accompanies. Since the purpose of the introductory rites is to prepare the people for the celebration it is appropriate that the entrance song refer to the liturgical season, the feast being celebrated, or the reading of the day. The theme of the entrance antiphon given in the missal is a helpful guideline in the choice of the entrance song.

Veneration of altar
Priest and ministers greet the altar by bowing profoundly. Priest, and any ordained ministers, kiss the altar. Priest may incense the altar, walking around it (*IG 27, 84, 85*).

Salutation of people
From the chair. Purpose: To remind the faithful that the Lord is present among them (*IG 28*). The priest should keep in mind the profound scriptural and theological content of these short greetings.

Introduction to the celebration
After the salutation, the priest may very briefly (*brevissimis verbis*) introduce the Mass (*IG 29*).

Penitential rite
May be adapted to the occasion and to the varying circumstances of the community (*EP 14*).

Kyrie
Is sung (or recited) here unless already included in the penitential rite. Since it is the people's cry for mercy it should normally be sung by everybody. Each acclamation is normally made twice, but because of the nature of the language, the music, or other circumstances, the number may be greater or short verses inserted (*IG 30*). It may be well on occasion to use the ancient Greek *Kyrie eleison*; this is a link with our past as well as with the Eastern rite liturgies. Since it is part of the preparatory rites, the *Kyrie* should not be unduly long or elaborate.

Gloria
The *Gloria* may be sung by the choir, the people, or both in alternation. The introductory character of this part of the celebration should be kept in mind, as in the case of the *Kyrie*.

Opening prayer or collect
"Let us pray" is an invitation to the people to pray in silence for a few moments, reflecting that they are in God's presence. Each person formulates his own intentions mentally (*IG 32, 88*). The long conclusion is used; this should be prayed with care, in such a way as to evoke a firm response *Amen* from the congregation.

Liturgy of the word
When the scriptures are read in the church God himself speaks to the people, and Christ, present in his word, proclaims his Gospel (*IG 9*). The readings, therefore, should be listened to

with respect. In them God's word is addressed to all men of every era (*IG 9*).

Because of the reverence due to the sacred text the reader should read from the lectionary, or other proper liturgical book, and not from a missalette or slip of paper.

Arrangement of readings

Sundays and certain feasts have three readings. These teach God's plan for salvation. On weekdays, unless a solemnity or feast occurs, the readings assigned to the particular day should normally be used. The continuous reading during the week, however, is sometimes interrupted by the occurrence of a feast or particular celebration. In this case the priest should consider in advance the entire week's readings; he may either combine readings so that none will be omitted, or decide which readings are to be preferred (*IG 318, 319*).

Introduction to the readings

A brief introduction to the readings may be given (*IG 11*). This may take the form of an aptly worded sentence or two designed to arouse the congregation's attention, and to help them to listen with profit to the message Christ is about to speak to them. (The captions given in the lectionary do not serve adequately as "introductions", nor were they intended to.)

Responsorial Psalm

Having listened to the word of God in the first reading, the people ponder it in their hearts and express their response to it in the Responsorial Psalm.

The psalm verses are sung from the ambo by a cantor. The people listen, and respond with the refrain. If it is not possible to sing the psalm appointed for the day, a judicious choice may be made from the lectionary, keeping in mind that the psalm should have some bearing on the reading that precedes it. The music for the refrain should be simple enough for the average person to be able to learn it, having heard it once or twice (*Notitiae*, February 1975, pp 59-60).

If the Responsorial Psalm is not sung but spoken, the reader should refrain from prompting the people's response with the repeated exclamation "response". A change in tempo and pitch can be just as effective and far more dignified.

Gospel acclamation

The moment of proclamation of the Gospel is the point towards which the earlier part of the celebration tends. The people stand and acclaim the presence of Christ in his word by singing "Alleluia". This acclamation, of its nature, should be sung, i.e. proclaimed in stylised fashion ("Certissime canendae sunt acclamationes" — *Notitiae*, May 1975). If it is not sung it may be omitted (*IG 39*). During Lent another chant is used. If not sung it may be omitted. A procession, with the carrying of the gospel book, thurible and candles, may take place during the singing of the Alleluia (*IG 94*). This can help to emphasise the reverence which should accompany the reading of the Gospel (*IG 35*).

Gospel

The reading of the Gospel should be done with great reverence (*IG 35*).

Homily

The homily is a living explanation of the word. It increases the effectiveness of the word, and is an integral part of the service (*IG 9*). It explains the word in view of the total celebration, and in terms of daily life (*EP 15*). The homily should develop some point of the readings or of another text from the Ordinary of the Mass of the day. The homilist should keep in mind the mystery being celebrated, and the needs of the particular community (*IG 41*).

In the liturgy of the word Christ speaks to the people. It is for the homilist to explain and actualise the text, to apply it to the needs of the worshipping community, to let them hear the voice of Christ. It is the task of the homilist to help the people hear what Christ is saying, to absorb his message, and to reform their lives in the light of that message and with the strength of the Eucharist.

The homily is to be given on Sundays and holy days of obligation at all Masses which are celebrated with a congregation. It is recommended on other days, especially on the weekdays of Advent, Lent, and the Easter season as well as on other feasts and occasions when the people come to church in large numbers (*IG 42*). Even one or two sentences can be effective, especially if they lead into a moment of silent reflection on the readings.

The homily may be preached from the ambo or the chair (*IG 97*).

Creed

Through the *Creed*, the Profession of Faith, the people profess their adherence to God's word, which they have heard in the readings and homily (*IG 33, 43*). It is also a time for the people to recall the teachings of the faith before they begin the celebration of the Eucharist (*IG 43*).

Prayer of the faithful

Here the people exercise their priestly function by interceding for all mankind (*IG 45*), in response to the word of God (*EP 16*). Hence the importance of these prayers. To be effective, the petitions, which are made for the needs of all men, should win the assent of the people gathered locally. Insight and a certain freedom should go into their composition (*EP 16*). As a rule the sequence of intentions is: for the needs of the Church; for public authorities and the salvation of the world; for those oppressed by any need; for the local community (*IG 46*). The priest invites the people to pray, with a brief introduction. After the intentions he says the concluding prayer. The congregation makes its petition either by a common response after each intention, or by silent prayer (*IG 47*).

Spontaneous unprepared interventions during the prayer of the faithful, whether they come from priest or people, can indicate a poverty of content and hesitancy of expression which do not make for effective celebration.

Liturgy of the Eucharist

At the Last Supper Christ instituted the paschal sacrifice and meal, offering his body and blood to the Father, under the species of bread and wine. In this meal the sacrifice of the cross is continually made present in the Church when the priest, representing Christ, carries out what the Lord did and handed over to his disciples to do in his memory. Christ took bread and the cup, gave thanks, broke, and gave to his disciples, saying: "Take and eat, this is my body. Take and drink, this is my blood. Do this in memory of me." The Church has arranged the celebration of the Eucharistic liturgy to correspond to these words and actions of Christ:

1. In the preparation of the gifts, bread and wine and water are brought to the altar, the same elements which Christ used.
2. The eucharistic prayer is the hymn of thanksgiving to God for the whole work of salvation; the offerings become the body and blood of Christ.
3. The breaking of the one bread is a sign of the unity of the faithful, and in communion they receive the body and blood of Christ as the apostles did from his hands (*IG 48*).

Preparation of the gifts

Preparation of altar: Corporal, purificator, chalice and missal are placed on the altar, which up to this point should have on it only the altar cloth; the candles, which may, alternatively, be placed near the altar; and the cross, which, again, may be placed, alternatively, somewhere in the vicinity of the altar (*IG 269, 270*). The cluttering of the altar with unnecessary objects, e.g. charts, should be avoided.

The gifts, bread and wine: Bread must be wheaten, and unleavened. It should look like natural food, and should therefore, even though unleavened and traditional in form, be made in such a way that the priest can break it and distribute it to at least some of the faithful (*IG 283*). The wine must be natural and pure, made from the fruit of the vine. It should not be mixed with any foreign substance (*IG 284*).

Procession with gifts: This is desirable and fitting. Other gifts for the Church and the poor may also be carried in the procession. These are to be placed in a suitable place, but not on the altar (*IG 49, 101*).

Prayers: The prayers, during the preparation of the gifts, up to and excluding the *Orate Fratres*, should be said *secreto* (i.e. inaudibly). But, if there is no chant, the priest may say the blessing prayers, over the bread and wine, aloud, and only these (*Ordo Missae*).

Song: The procession with the gifts may be accompanied by the offertory song, which continues at least until the gifts are placed on the altar (*IG 50*). The song need not speak of bread and wine or offering. Its purpose is to accompany the procession. Any appropriate song of praise, rejoicing, thanks, etc. in keeping with the season may be used. Song is not always necessary, or even desirable at this point. A few moments of quiet can be a fitting sequel to the liturgy of the word, and a fitting preparation to highlight the great eucharistic prayer; for this reason it may be well at times to replace the offertory song with a few moments of silence, or some quiet instrumental music.

Incensation: The gifts and altar may be incensed (*IG 51*).

Eucharistic prayer

The eucharistic prayer is the centre and the high point of the entire celebration. The meaning of the prayer is that the whole congregation joins Christ in acknowledging the works of God, and in offering sacrifice (*IG 54*). The spirit of the eucharistic prayer as "praise of the wonderful works of God" (*IG 54*) is expressed most effectively when priest and people sing the parts allocated to them. Music reveals depths in the liturgical text which may be lost if it is just spoken. This is particularly true of the people's acclamations.

The use of song during the eucharistic prayer

The singing of the dialogue before the Preface emphasises that a new and important part of the celebration is now beginning and that the priest is praising God with the enthusiastic support of the community.

The sung proclamation of the praise of God in the Preface calls for the singing of the *Sanctus* by the people. The *Sanctus* should never be taken over by a choir to the exclusion of the congregation. A glance at *Isaiah 6:3-4* and *Luke 19:37-40*, from which the text of the *Sanctus* is drawn, will show that it is intended to be a resounding chorus of joyful praise involving "the whole multitude" (*Luke 19:37*).

At the memorial acclamation the priest invites the people to *proclaim* the mystery of faith. Music adds a dimension of affirmation to this proclamation of the central belief of Christians. The nature of this acclamation demands that all should sing it.

The singing of the doxology "Through him, with him," etc. by the priest emphasises its character of praise. The people express the fact that they have made this praise their own by singing "Amen". The prolongation and repetition of this short word which is made possible through song allows the people to reflect on the meaning of this great Amen and on its implications for the daily living of the Christian life.

The chief elements of the eucharistic prayer are these:

(a) Thanksgiving (expressed especially in the preface): in the name of the entire people of God, the priest praises the Father and gives him thanks for the work of salvation or for some special aspect of it in keeping with the day, feast or season.

(b) Acclamation: united with the angels, the congregation sings or recites the *Sanctus*. This acclamation forms part of the eucharistic prayer, and all the people join with the priest in singing or reciting it.

(c) Epiclesis: in special invocations the Church calls on God's power and asks that the gifts offered by men may be consecrated, that is, become the body and blood of Christ and that the victim may become a source of salvation for those who are to share in communion.

(d) Narrative of the institution and consecration: in the words and actions of Christ, the sacrifice he instituted at the Last Supper is celebrated, when under the appearances of bread and wine he offered his body and blood, gave them to his apostles to eat and drink, and commanded them to carry on this mystery.

(e) Anamnesis: in fulfilment of the command received from Christ through the apostles, the Church keeps his memorial by recalling especially his passion, resurrection and ascension.

(f) Offering: in this memorial, the Church — and in particular the Church here and now assembled — offers the victim to the Father in the Holy Spirit. The Church's intention is that the faithful not only offer the spotless victim but also learn to offer themselves and daily to be drawn into ever more perfect union, through Christ the Mediator, with the Father and with each other, so that at last God may be all in all.

(g) Intercessions: the intercessions make it clear that the Eucharist is celebrated in communion with the whole Church of heaven and earth, and that the offering is made for the Church and all its members, living and dead, who are called to share in the salvation and redemption acquired by the body and blood of Christ.

(h) Final doxology: the praise of God is expressed in the doxology which is confirmed and concluded by the acclamation of the people.

Choice of eucharistic prayer

The various eucharistic prayers express different aspects of what the Church believes and wishes to say about the Eucharist. Priests therefore should not confine themselves to the same eucharistic prayer, but should make use of the variety which the Church offers (that is the four eucharistic prayers of the missal, together with the eucharistic prayers for children and for Masses of reconciliation, and any other eucharistic prayers which the Church might possibly approve of at a future date). If the faithful are given the opportunity, in this way, of hearing all the eucharistic prayers from time to time they will eventually come to know them thoroughly and will find them a rich source of catechesis on the mystery of the Eucharist.

1. Eucharistic Prayer I, the Roman Canon, may always be used. It is more appropriate on days with special variable parts: *Communicantes, Hanc igitur*; on the feasts of apostles or saints mentioned in it; and on Sundays.

2. Eucharistic Prayer II is suitable for weekdays and special circumstances.

3. Eucharistic Prayer III is particularly suited for Sundays and feasts.

4. Eucharistic Prayer IV is most suitable for a congregation which has a comparatively good grasp of scripture (*IG 322*). However, pastoral practice is showing that Eucharistic Prayer IV is well within the grasp of our average congregation, and can provide people and even children with a clear picture of the whole plan of salvation. Note: The preface of Eucharistic Prayer IV is fixed.

The celebrant alone should proclaim the eucharistic prayer. The people should listen in silent reverence, and share in it by making the acclamations, especially with song: Sanctus, Proclamation of Faith and the Great Amen (*IG 55h, 19*).

Choice of prefaces
Use should be made of the wide choice of prefaces in the revised missal. Through them the different prefaces, different aspects of the mystery of salvation can be emphasised, and richer themes of thanksgiving made available (*EP 8*).

Introducing the eucharistic prayer
The celebrant may briefly introduce the eucharistic prayer (*IG 11*). He, may, for example, suggest motives of thanksgiving

suited to the particular congregation (*EP 8*).

Communion rite
Through Holy Communion the faithful perfect that communion with God and among themselves which should be the fruit of participation in the sacrifice of the Eucharist (*EM 12*). They should receive at the proper time, during the actual Mass, and from bread consecrated at that same Mass (*EM 33a, IG 56h*). Communicants should abstain from food and drink, with the exception of water, for one hour before Communion[1]. They are encouraged to receive from the chalice on the occasions permitted[2]; in that form the sign of the eucharistic banquet appears more clearly, the intention of Christ that the new eternal covenant be ratified in his blood is better expressed, and the eucharistic banquet is more clearly seen to prefigure the heavenly banquet (*IG 240*). The faithful should be instructed on the meaning of communion from the chalice, and on the Church's teaching that the true Sacrament, Christ, whole and entire, is received even when communion is from one species only.

The Lord's Prayer
This prayer belongs to the congregation. It should not be sung by a soloist or choir (*Notitiae*, January 1975). Adopting the principle that not all the singable parts of the Mass need necessarily be sung, it is better to say the Our Father than for a small group within the congregation to sing it.

Rite of peace
Here the people may express their love for one another through an appropriate gesture, and beg for peace and unity in the Church and with all mankind (*IG 56b*). The form of the gesture and the way in which it is carried out should respect the nature and purpose of the rite. Informal greetings and casual enquiries are not appropriate. Neither are embraces or more

[1] See exceptions for the infirm etc. page 108.
[2] Listed on page 166.

demonstrative signs of affection. One gesture which works well is the double handshake in one or other form. Another appropriate sign is the brief silent pause during which the people, at the invitation of the priest (or deacon) reflect upon the meaning of forgiveness and peace. The old-style "kiss of peace", from the Solemn High Mass of pre-conciliar days, continues to be an attractive and expressive gesture, especially among concelebrants.

Breaking of bread

This gesture shows that in communion, we who are many are made one body in the one bread of life (*IG 56c*). At least some of the faithful should receive from the same large host as the priest (*IG 283*).

Agnus Dei

This chant accompanies the breaking of bread, and may be repeated as often as is necessary while the bread is being broken (*IG 56e*). The words may be sung by the entire congregation, or alternated between cantor, choir and congregation.

Silent preparation

Priest and people prepare for communion by praying quietly. The commingling prayer and the prayer *Lord Jesus Christ* are said *secreto*, i.e. inaudibly (*IG 196*).

Communion procession

The faithful are recommended to approach the sacred table in an ordered fraternal procession (*EM 34*). The communion song, which they sing as they walk in procession to the altar, expresses the spiritual union of the communicants, and shows their joy and brotherly bond in Christ as they partake in the sacred banquet (*IG 56*).

Suitable songs for the communion procession would refer to the feast being celebrated, the liturgical season, or to themes of joy, praise or fraternity. The communion antiphon in the missal is a guideline in the choice of a suitable communion song. For practical reasons, the responsorial method is most appropriate as a means to congregational involvement.

Hymns of adoration of the Blessed Sacrament do not necessarily correspond to the spirit of the communion procession, and may be more suited to devotions to the Eucharist outside Mass (cf. *MS 36, 46*).

Silent prayer

After communion the priest and people may spend some time in silent prayer (*pro opportunitate*, *IG 56*). A hymn or other song of praise may be sung (*si placet*, *IG 56*). Announcements and any concluding comments may be made before the dismissal (*IG 11, 139*).

Concluding rite

The concluding rite may be expanded, at the discretion of the priest, by drawing from the rich collection of "Solemn Blessings" and "Prayers over the People" contained in the missal (cf. *IG 57*).

Mass without a congregation

Mass celebrated by a priest with only one minister, to assist and make the responses, follows in general the rite of Mass with a congregation. Detailed directions for a Mass with only one minister are given in the *General Instruction of the Missal, 209 ff*. Points of particular note are:

1. The introductory rites take place at the altar, not at the chair.
2. The concluding rite is carried out as at Mass with a congregation, but the dismissal is omitted.

Mass should not be celebrated without a minister except in serious necessity. In this case the greetings and the blessing at the end of Mass are omitted.

CONCELEBRATED MASS

Introduction

Concelebration of the Eucharist has existed in the Church from antiquity. In every type of Mass, no matter how simple, all the qualities and properties are to be found which necessarily form part of the holy sacrifice. The unity of the sacrifice of the cross, the unity of the priesthood, and the unity of God's people, are properties of unique importance. Every Mass is the celebration of that sacrifice by which the Church lives and grows continuously (*LG 26*), and in which its own nature is especially manifested (*SC 41*).

Concelebration of the Eucharist aptly demonstrates the unity of the sacrifice and of the priesthood. Whenever the faithful take an active part, the unity of the people of God is strikingly manifested, particularly if the bishop presides (*EM 47*). The Eucharist is the sacrifice in which the unity of the Church becomes real in a communal and hierarchical celebration.

Concelebration both symbolises and strengthens the brotherly bond of the priesthood, because in virtue of the sacred ordination and mission which they have in common, all priests are bound together in an intimate brotherhood (*EM 47; LG 28*).

Concelebration is that liturgical action in which several priests act together with one will and one voice, by the power of the same priesthood and *in persona Christi*; together they consecrate and offer the one sacrifice in one sacrificial act, and together they participate in it (*DG*).

The rite of concelebration expresses and vividly inculcates truths of great moment for the spiritual and pastoral lives of priests and the Christian formation of the faithful (*DG*).

Concelebration does not involve a simultaneous celebration of many priests who say Mass separately. It is not a juxtaposition of priests by way of speech, as separate units, but every concelebration presupposes a real unity, a college, a community of celebrants, a unity which takes shape in the bishop as main celebrant. Concelebrants are related to the bishop "like strings to the harp" as Ignatius of Antioch says to the Ephesians (*4:1*). Concelebration presupposes a structured unity in which one takes the leadership, and the others join in unison. One eucharistic celebration is performed by many.

This coming together of a college of priests is meaningful since all members represent the one High Priest, Jesus Christ and, in the case of the eucharistic celebration, offer the one complete sacrifice of the cross. The totality is carried by the one salvific reality, which cannot be multiplied, Jesus Christ the Lord. Numerical multiplication makes sense primarily in relation to the distinctness of time, place, and communities of faithful.

Both Pope Pius XII, speaking to the Assisi Congress in 1956, and the Holy Office, in a reply of 1957, have stated that concelebration is not possible unless the words of consecration are spoken jointly by the concelebrants. The common pronunciation of the words of consecration is the sign that one, as priest, actively participates in this sacrifice and actually partakes in this concrete sacramental representation. However, the pronunciation of these words should not be seen only as consecratory, but also as the action of this college of priests in the communal performance of the sacramental offering.

It is fitting that priests participate in the Eucharist, and exercise the order proper to them, by celebrating or concelebrating, and not by limiting themselves to communicating like the laity (*EM 43; CM* prologue). Where this full form of participation is not possible, then priests can and should receive Holy Communion on those occasions where concelebration would be permitted, or where Holy Communion twice in the same day is permitted.

The ritual of concelebration

Preparation: Every liturgical celebration should be prepared with care, and with the cooperation of those concerned (*IG 73*). Those in charge should see to it that concelebration is performed with dignity and true piety (*CM 3b*), according to the norms of the missal. Each part of the Mass should be celebrated as its nature demands, tasks and functions should be clearly defined, and attention paid to the singing and to the moments of silence (*CM 3a*).

The regulation of the discipline of concelebration in the diocese pertains to the bishop (*SC 57,2i*), though the competent superior has authority to judge whether concelebration is opportune, and to give permission for it (*IG 155; RSCM 3*). The *General Instruction on the Missal*, *n.153*, indicates those occasions on which concelebration is permitted, and *n.158* gives the occasions when priests may celebrate or concelebrate more than once in the day.

All that is said in the documents about the importance and symbolism of concelebration for communities is valid also for those occasions on which priests come together for any cause whatever (*quacumque de causa insimul conveniunt*). To all such occasions, the faculty granted by *n.158* of the *General Instruction* is extended. Whenever there is a gathering of priests, for any special occasion, all those who are bound to celebrate for the pastoral good of the faithful may concelebrate with their brothers (*Notitiae*, November 1972, p.331), because fraternal concelebration by priests symbolises and strengthens the links which unite them with one another, and which unite the community (*CM 1*).

Priests who celebrate Mass for the good of the faithful, and who concelebrate at another Mass may not accept a stipend for the concelebrated Mass (*CM 3b*).

A large host should be used for concelebration. Care should be taken that, in keeping with traditional usage, it should be of such a shape and appearance as befits so great a sacrament (*EM 48; IG 281ff.*).

Celebration:

At a concelebrated Mass, if neither deacon nor any other ministers are available, their duties are undertaken by one of the concelebrants.

Ideally, concelebrants should be fully vested, but for a good reason the concelebrants may omit the chasuble (*IG 161*). The principal concelebrant always wears a chasuble. On no account should a priest celebrate Mass, or join in a concelebrated Mass, without the required vestments.

If a large number of priests are concelebrating it would be helpful to have a master of ceremonies.

Having made the customary reverence, and kissed the altar, the concelebrants go to the places prepared for them (*IG 162*). Nobody may join in a concelebration once the Mass has begun (*IG 156*).

From the beginning of Mass up to the end of the rite of Preparation of the Gifts, the concelebrants remain at their places unless one or other of them has been assigned a specific function (*IG 164ff*). The homily is normally given by the principal concelebrant (*IG 165*).

When the rite of the Preparation of the Gifts is complete, the concelebrants approach the altar and stand around it. They should not be in the way of other ministers who may have duties to perform, and should not obscure the people's view of the celebration (*IG 167*).

In those parts of the eucharistic prayer which are to be said by all the concelebrants together, these should employ a tone of voice quiet enough for the voice of the principal to be heard above them all (*IG 170*). An ancient document expresses it thus: "ut vox pontificis valentius audiatur" (*Ordo Romanus III*).

During the eucharistic prayer, when the concelebrants first pray together (at the first Epiclesis), they outstretch their hands towards the offerings (*IG 174a*); and after the consecration (during the anamesis and second Epiclesis), they pray together with outstretched arms. *Nn. 171-191* of the *General Instruction* indicate how the four eucharistic prayers are proclaimed at concelebration. As different parts of the eucharistic prayer are proclaimed either by the president, by one of the concelebrants, or by all together, special attention should be given to the tone of voice and to the pace (*EP 7*). The eucharistic prayer is the high point of the whole celebration, so "dignity and true piety" apply here in a unique way.

The concelebrants exchange the sign of peace with one

another (*IG 194*); and the norms for the rite of Communion are contained in *nn. 200ff.* of the *General Instruction*.

At the end of Mass only the principal celebrant kisses the altar. The concelebrants make the customary reverence (*IG 208*).

Every priest retains the right to celebrate Mass alone, and facilities for such celebration should be provided (*SC 57,2ii; EM 47; CM 3*). Such a celebration of the Eucharist without participation by the faithful is also "the centre of the entire Church and the heart of priestly existence" (Synod of Bishops, *De Sacerdotio Ministerali, 2:3; CM 3c*). However, a "single" Mass may not be celebrated in the church in which concelebration is actually taking place.

A concelebrated Mass should be so organised and celebrated that it will be clearly evident to all who are participating, that this whole eucharistic celebration is the pre-eminent manifestation of the Church as "a chosen race, a royal priesthood, a holy nation, God's own people" (*1 Pet 2:9*).

CHILDREN AT MASS

The Church, following its Master, loves little children. It cannot leave them to themselves. If over the years children find the Mass scarcely intelligible spiritual harm may follow. For this reason Mass should be adapted to their particular needs. The principles for such adaptation are given in the *Directory on Masses for Children* issued by the Congregation for Divine Worship on 1 November 1973, and in the Introduction to *Eucharistic Prayers for Masses with Children* issued by the same Congregation on 1 November 1974. The aim of these documents is to help children who have not yet entered the period of pre-adolescence to participate fully and actively in the Eucharist.

These documents, while stressing the need for adaptation, stress also the importance of orientating children's Masses towards Masses for adults, in the sense that through their own

Masses children should be led towards participating effectively in Masses for adults. For this reason adaptations are to be avoided which would result in too great a difference between Masses with children and Masses with adults. Moreover, the participation of at least some adults is desirable at children's Masses; the witness of adults can have a profound effect upon the children, especially when they are present not as monitors, but praying with the children and helping them.

The *Directory* clearly defines the areas in which adaptation is possible in children's Masses. The general structure of the Mass, the liturgy of the word and the liturgy of the Eucharist, should always be maintained, as should some rites to open and conclude the celebration. The following should never be adapted: the acclamations and the responses of the faithful to the greeting of the priest; the Lord's Prayer, and the trinitarian formula at the end of the final blessing. A resumé of the various directives is given below.

The liturgy of the word

A children's Mass should have at least one Bible reading. Any suitable readings from the lectionary or Bible may be chosen. Difficult sentences may be omitted, provided that the overall sense is unimpaired. If one reading only is chosen, it should be a Gospel reading. It is commendable to use those versions of scripture already approved for catechetical purposes. Children read the First Reading, and where the Gospel lends itself, the children can take different parts as is provided for the reading of the Passion. In all children's Masses a homily explaining the word of God is important. The homily may take the form of a dialogue with the children and may be given by the celebrant or one of the adults present.

The liturgy of the Eucharist

The eucharistic prayer is of the greatest importance in the Eucharist celebrated with children, because it is the high point of the celebration. Much depends on the manner in which the

priest proclaims this prayer and in which the children take part
by listening and making their acclamations.

The disposition of mind required for this central part of the
celebration, the calm and reverence with which everything is
done, should make the children as attentive as possible.

Only those eucharistic prayers which are approved by the
Holy See for use at adult or children's Masses may be used.

The celebrant

Much will depend on the personal preparation of the celebrant,
and on his manner of presiding and speaking. He should speak
in such a way as to be understood by the children, while at the
same time avoiding any childish way of speaking. It is his
responsibility to make the celebration festive, fraternal and
meditative.

Participation

Children, in order to receive the word and celebrate the
Eucharist, need to become as involved as possible both in body,
through words, song, gesture and music, and in mind, through
silence, reflection, listening and sharing.

Singing and music

Singing, an asset to any celebration, has a special place in
children's Masses. Acclamations should be sung rather than
said. A psalm or psalm-type hymn, or simple Alleluia should
form part of the liturgy of the word. The *Directory* permits the
rewriting of official texts, such as the *Gloria, Sanctus* and *Agnus
Dei*, to allow them to be sung to appropriate musical settings.
Instrumental accompaniment and recorded music can also have
a place in children's Masses.

Gesture and movement

Gesture and movement are to be highly recommended in
children's Masses. *Processions* are encouraged especially at
entrance, gospel, preparation of gifts, communion.

Visuals
The value of visuals is also stressed, especially the children's own creations, illustrating the readings, homily and themes for prayer. Use of these in the actual celebration is encouraged.

Silence
At different times in the Mass (for example after communion or even after the homily), children are to be helped to pray *silently* to God in their hearts.

The place of celebration
The principle is established that the church is the primary place for a eucharistic celebration with children. A space within the church could be selected to suit the number of children participating. Where this is not possible or suitable, another room may be chosen, one which is suitable and "worthy of the dignity of the Mass". Children are encouraged to prepare and decorate the place of celebration and to prepare the gifts.

Children at Sunday Mass
The children who are present at a parish Mass must never be allowed to feel neglected because of their inability to participate in or understand what is going on. A few special words may be said to them during the greeting and introduction. Simple words and simple ideas should be used. Part of the homily may be specifically addressed to the children. Here again simplicity and brevity are important. One central idea to which the celebrant returns frequently will be a great help to the children and will make them feel part of the celebration. A final word may be spoken to them at the end of Mass.

Infants can be a problem at Mass. The *Directory* suggests that if possible they should be cared for by parish helpers and brought to the church for the final blessing of the Mass. Another helpful suggestion is that there be a special adapted form of the liturgy of the word for children, in a separate place. The children return to the church for the liturgy of the Eucharist.

We are reminded in the *Directory* that "the Church whose Master took the little children in his arms and blessed them" cannot be content to leave children to their own devices. We are asked to share our faith with them, to give them an experience of the Eucharist and to help them live this celebration in their lives.

Resumé of directives from *Directory on Masses for Children*[1]

Directives apply to pre-adolescents and to mentally and physically handicapped (*6*).

One may put infants in separate room, bringing them in for blessing at end (*16*).

Give tasks to as many children as possible, from preparing room to reading lessons (*22*).

Choose suitable space in church, or elsewhere (*25*).

Celebrant's contribution crucial — setting festive, friendly and prayerful tone, speaking directly and simply to children when inviting them to penance, sign of peace, etc. (*23*).

Get the children in on preparation of Mass (*29*).

Get the children to sing and to play musical instruments, but not so as to overshadow the singing (*30, 32*).

Recorded music is permissible, but according to hierarchy's directives (*32*).

Processions are recommended, at entrance, gospel, offertory, communion (*34*).

Visual aids may be used, including pictures done by the children themselves for homily, prayer of the faithful, etc. (*35*).

Silent prayer or meditation suggested after communion or homily (*37*).

The following elements never to be changed: acclamations and responses of the faithful to the priest's greetings, the Lord's Prayer, the trinitarian formula in priest's blessing at the end (*38*).

[1] Based by kind permission on a resumé given with *Doctrine and Life*.

Mass for children, step by step

Opening rite

a] One may omit one or more of the following and amplify another, but in rotation (*40*): entrance hymn or antiphon, Sign of the Cross and greeting, penitential act, *Gloria* (when prescribed); an approved popular adaptation may be sung in its place (*31*).

b] One must always have the opening prayer, but celebrant may choose any prayer from Roman Missal, simplifying it if necessary, but preserving its meaning and genre (*40, 51*).

The Readings

What is permitted: omission of all save Gospel readings (*41*); substitution of any reading(s) from lectionary or Bible for reading(s) appointed (*41*); omission of difficult sentences, provided overall sense unimpaired (*41*); paraphrases to be avoided, but one may employ version sanctioned for catechetical use (*43*); children may do speaking parts in a reading, as in the Passion (*47*).

The homily

The *homily* may be given by a lay person, with the consent of the parish priest or rector (*23*).
Dialogue homily permitted (*48*), e.g. preacher asking questions, children replying (*22*).

Creed

Approved popular adaption may be sung in its place (*31*).
Apostles' Creed may be used instead of Nicene Creed (*49*).

Preface

Before the preface celebrant may insert additional reasons for giving thanks i.e. reasons closer to children's experience (*22*).

Sanctus

An approved popular adaptation may be sung in its place (*31*).

Eucharistic prayers

One must use one of the four given in the Roman Missal unless the Church makes other provision (*52*), as has happened with the approved eucharistic prayers for children.

The rites before communion

The rites may be shortened, but the Lord's Prayer, the breaking of bread and the invitation to communion must never be omitted (*53*).

The *Agnus Dei*: approved popular adaptation may be sung in its place (*31*).

Holy communion and after

Children to be tranquil and recollected (*54*).

Few words before the final blessing can help to show connection between liturgy and life (*54*).

THE SMALL GROUP MASS

Introduction

The community celebration of the Eucharist on Sundays and holy days in the presence of the bishop or in the parish assembly is the sign and instrument of unity among all men, and above all, of the unity of the Church with Christ. Pastoral activity is directed to this end. This can be furthered by liturgical celebrations for particular groups, where their special needs and circumstances can be catered for, where their common spiritual or apostolic commitment can be enriched and where they can acquire a more profound personal formation. This should inspire them with a sense of mission and make them more active and effective members of the wider Christian community. The vitality of such groups comes from their common search for Christian truth and their common desire to live according to it.

Celebration of the Eucharist for small groups

The celebration of the Eucharist for small groups should be

organised and directed in a wise and prudent way so as to promote respect for the sacred mysteries and the spiritual good of those taking part. Such celebration should be seen as an important element of the whole pastoral activity of the parish and a privileged occasion for developing the liturgical attitudes and practice of the people.

A *small group* consists of a restricted number of people, say not more than twenty-five; though this is a relative matter. There is a certain type of personal, individual relationship between the members of the group.

Kinds of groups

a) Meetings: retreats, study-groups, lay apostolate, etc.

b) Certain communities: seminaries, sodalities, hospitals, etc.

c) Pastoral groups: visitation, stations, anointing of the sick, death, street-groups, etc.

d) Special interest groups: cultural groups, leisure groups, workers, professional groups.

e) Groups based on common characteristics: youth, aged, married couples, etc.

f) Groups based on family events: new house, arrival or departure in the family, etc.

Value of this type of celebration

Through the formation and the prayer activity: it helps the faith of the participants; integrates them into the community of believers; fosters their apostolic commitment — on condition that there is a close link with the community parish liturgy.

Celebration of the Eucharist

The nature of the Eucharist must be respected and so influence every aspect of the celebration. The norms of *IG, EM* are to be observed.

The small-group Mass is complementary to the Sunday parish celebration and should lead to a fuller and more active participation in that community celebration. Hence, group

Masses should not take place on Sundays and holy days of obligation (*IMSG 10a*).

The particular nature of each group calls for adaptations to suit the spiritual good of the members. These should be made in consultation with those taking part.

Full advantage should be taken of the small group and their proximity to the priest and altar to deepen their understanding of the Eucharist and to enable them to participate fully and actively in the celebration.

Conditions for the celebration of the Eucharist

If the priest celebrant is not the parish priest he should inform the parish priest beforehand, who is to make a report to the bishop on the small-group Masses celebrated in his parish (*IMSG 10b*).

The laws of the eucharistic fast are to be observed. If there is a meal it should not immediately precede the Mass and should be completely distinct from it.

The celebration should not take place too late at night (*IMSG 10e*).

At family celebrations those who reasonably ask to attend should be allowed to do so.

Place of celebration

(a) A church or oratory.

(b) Any place worthy of the Blessed Eucharist and suitably prepared, with the permission of the Ordinary, e.g. hall, private house, workshop, classroom, etc. The choice is to be made on pastoral grounds (*IMSG 4*).

(c) In choosing a place for the celebration great care should be taken to avoid favouring one group more than another or one family more than another.

(d) Outside a church or oratory Mass may be celebrated on a table, covered with a clean cloth and corporal. There is no obligation to use an altarstone (*IG 260, 265; IMSG 11b*).

(e) The place should be decorated to express the aspect of

joyful celebration and so arranged as to allow for proximity to the altar and full participation.

Material requisites

The bread to be used for the Eucharist is unleavened, the only kind allowed in the Latin Church, in the form used in other Masses (*IMSG 10d, cf. IG 282, 283*).

The furnishings of the altar, the sacred vestments, vessels and vestments should be in accordance with the prescriptions of *IG 268-270; 290-296*, and *IMSG 11b*.

Organisation

So that the celebration of the Eucharist may be better adapted to the conditions of persons and places the different elements are organised in a suitable way, taking into account the general norms and the following principles (*IMSG 6*):

(a) Encourage as much participation as possible according to the particular circumstances and the possibilities of the group (*IMSG 6a*).

(b) The celebration may be preceded by a period of meditation on Sacred Scripture or spiritual instruction, according to the nature of the group (*IMSG 6b*).

(c) Apart from the opening monition the celebrant may present briefly the liturgy of the word before the readings, and the liturgy of the Eucharist before the preface. He may speak before the dismissal; but he should not intervene during the eucharistic prayer (*IMSG 6c*).

(d) Taking into account what is indicated in f. and h. below, and with the exception of the interventions of a commentator, the faithful should not intervene with exhortations, considerations or similar things (*IMSG 6d*).

(e) In the liturgy of the word, according to the circumstances, one may choose texts better adapted to the particular celebration, provided they are taken from an approved lectionary (*IMSG 6e*).

(f) The readings which precede the Gospel may be proclaimed

by one of the participants (male or female); the Gospel is to be
proclaimed by a priest or deacon (*IMSG 6f*).

(g) In the homily the priest will recall the particular character
of this celebration and he will point out the link between the
group present and the local church and the universal church
(*IMSG 6g*).

(h) The universal prayer may be adapted to the particular
circumstances, while keeping its religious character. One
should not omit general intentions — for the Church, the
world, brothers in need and the assembly present. Those
present may add special intentions, prepared beforehand
(*IMSG 6h*).

Communion

Sacramental communion is the most perfect and complete form
of participation. The manner of receiving Holy Communion,
lawfully in use in each diocese, should be followed. The rules of
the *General Instruction on the Roman Missal* should be followed
for communion under both kinds (*IMSG 7; IG 240-243;
EM 32, 6, 41*).

Singing

Singing can be most effective at the small-group Mass. The
principles already given for the use of song at Mass apply here.

WORSHIP OF THE EUCHARIST OUTSIDE MASS

Worship of the reserved Eucharist

Purpose of reservation of the blessed Eucharist

The Blessed Eucharist is reserved outside of Mass:

(a) so that the faithful who cannot be present at the celebration
of Mass, especially the sick and the aged, can be united to
Christ and his sacrifice through sacramental communion;

(b) so that the faithful may adore our Lord Jesus Christ present in the sacrament.

Worship of the holy Eucharist

The reserved sacrament is truly Emmanuel, "God with us". In it Christ is present whole and entire, God and man, substantially and permanently, and is to be adored with the worship due to God.

The Church strongly encourages both private and public devotion to the holy Eucharist, and calls on pastors to foster such devotion among the faithful by word and example.

In arranging the forms of this worship pastors should take account of the liturgical seasons, so that devotions will harmonise with the liturgy, be in some way derived from it, and lead the people to it.

Essential link between worship of the Eucharist outside Mass and Mass itself

The Mass itself is the origin and purpose of the worship given to the blessed Eucharist outside Mass. This worship follows from the Mass, and directs the faithful back to the Mass itself. In worshipping Christ present in the Eucharist, therefore, the faithful should keep in mind that this presence derives from the sacrifice of the Mass and is directed towards both sacramental and spiritual communion. Thus through communion outside Mass the faithful are united both with the Lord's sacrifice and with the community of Christ's Church, and are assured of their loving support.

Prayer before the blessed Sacrament

"The devotion which leads the faithful to visit the blessed Sacrament draws them into an ever deeper participation in the paschal mystery. It leads them to respond gratefully to the gift of him who through his humanity constantly pours divine life into the members of his body. Dwelling with Christ our Lord they enjoy his intimate friendship and pour out their hearts before him for themselves and their dear ones, and pray for the peace and salvation of the world. They offer their entire lives with Christ to the Father in the holy Spirit, and receive in this wonderful exchange an increase of faith, hope and charity. Thus they nourish those right dispositions which enable them with all due devotion to celebrate the memorial of the Lord, and receive frequently the bread given us by the Father" (*DSC 80*).

Moreover, prayer before the blessed Sacrament prolongs the union with Christ which the faithful reach in Holy Communion. It renews the covenant which, in turn, impels them to maintain in their daily lives what they have received by faith and sacraments.

Catechesis

The faithful should be clearly instructed in the preceding points, which may be summarised as follows:

(a) In the reserved sacrament Jesus Christ our Lord and Saviour is present, and is to be worshipped with that worship which is due to God alone.

(b) The Mass itself is the origin and purpose of the worship given to the blessed Eucharist outside Mass whether in communion, prayer before the blessed Sacrament, Benediction, exposition or eucharistic processions.

Place of reservation

Directives on the place of reservation are given in *Building and Reorganisation of Churches*, the Pastoral Directory of the Irish Episcopal Commission for Liturgy (*Veritas* 1972).

The presence of the blessed Sacrament is to be indicated by an oil lamp or a lamp with a wax candle.

Exposition and Benediction of the blessed Sacrament

Exposition is a special and solemn form of reservation, and must be seen in its relation to the Mass. It stimulates the faithful to an awareness of the wonderful presence of Christ, and is an invitation to intimate union with him, a union which reaches its high point in sacramental communion.

For exposition of the blessed Sacrament in a monstrance four to six candles are lighted, and incense is used. For exposition with a ciborium at least two candles should be lighted, and incense may be used.

A simple genuflection is made in the presence of the blessed Sacrament, whether it is reserved in the tabernacle or exposed for adoration.

1] Solemn annual exposition

The solemn annual exposition of the blessed Sacrament continues the tradition of the Forty Hours' devotion. It is desirable that parishes and religious communities should have an extended period of solemn exposition of the blessed Sacrament once a year.

(a) Exposition may be interrupted if it is seen that an appropriate number of the faithful will not be present continuously. This should not be done more than twice a day, for example at midday and at night.

(b) To show that the presence of Christ in the blessed Sacrament derives from the Mass the period of solemn exposition is to begin with Mass, in which the host to be exposed is consecrated.

After the distribution of communion the host is to be exposed. The Mass ends with the prayer after communion. Before the priest leaves he may incense the blessed Sacrament.

(c) It is preferable that the monstrance be placed on the altar, but if a throne is used this should not be too high or too far away from the people, since Christ is present in the Eucharist to be with his people and to unite them to him. A ciborium may also be used.

(d) In the ordering of the exposition and in the decoration which accompanies it care must be taken not to obscure the desire of Christ, who instituted it above all as the food, healing and support of his people. Decoration in flowers, candles and lights should be restrained.

(e) While the blessed Sacrament is exposed the celebration of Mass in the same area of the Church is forbidden. Either the exposition is to be interrupted or Mass is to be celebrated in a chapel apart. In the latter case some of the faithful should remain in adoration.

(f) When exposition is interrupted this may be carried out in the following way. A priest or deacon, vested in an alb, or surplice and soutane, with a stole, replaces the blessed Sacrament in the tabernacle after a short period of adoration and a prayer with the worshippers. Later, at the time appointed, exposition takes place again in the same way.

(g) During the exposition there should be prayers, hymns and scripture readings to direct the people's attention to the worship of the Lord. Together with the readings a homily or short exhortations can help towards a better understanding of the eucharistic mystery. Ample time should be allowed for silent prayer.

2] Shorter periods of exposition and Benediction

In addition to the solemn annual exposition of the blessed Sacrament the Church highly recommends shorter periods of exposition with Benediction.

(a) During exposition reasonable time should be given for scripture readings, hymns, prayers as well as silent recollection. These should be chosen so as to direct the devotion of the faithful to Christ present in the blessed Sacrament.

(b) Exposition merely for the purpose of giving Benediction is forbidden.

Processions of the blessed Sacrament

In processions in which the blessed Sacrament is solemnly

carried through the streets to the singing of hymns, especially on the feast of *Corpus Christi*, the Christian people give public witness to their faith and devotion towards this sacrament.

However, it is for the local Ordinary to judge whether such processions are opportune in present-day circumstances, and to determine the time, place and manner of such processions, so that they may be conducted with dignity and without loss of reverence to the sacrament.

It is fitting that the procession begin following the Mass in which the host to be carried is consecrated. A procession may also take place, however, at the end of an extended period of public adoration.

4 Penance

GENERAL CATECHESIS

A sacrament of reconciliation

On the day of the Resurrection our Lord gave the power to remit sins to the community of his followers (*Jn 20: 22*f). On the cross he had become the source of victory over sin and of the presence of the Holy Spirit for all who would turn to him in hope. On that first Easter he not only brought these gifts to the disciples themselves, who had abandoned him, but he established their community as the abiding source of these graces for all who would wish to seek union with him through that community and to live by its life. The community of Christ's Church is where the way to reconciliation with God has been opened up for man (*OPI*).

The ministry of reconciliation

The "ministry of reconciliation" (*2 Cor 5:18*) is carried out by the Church in a number of ways. It is not restricted to the sacrament of Penance, still less to a single structure of that sacrament. Basic to all reconciliation is the proclamation of Christ crucified, with his victory over sin and his gift of the Holy Spirit for all who approach him with a living faith. Reconciliation is going on through the ministry of the word and of the sacraments. It is made manifest wherever a local community gathers in intercession for returning sinners and "seeks their conversion by its charity, example and prayer" (*LG 11, OP 8*). But the main occasion on which it is

94

experienced by those who are already baptised is the sacrament of Penance, for here we have a celebration especially dedicated to Christ's presence in his Church for sinners.

Reconciliation with the Church

In this sacramental mystery there is a twofold reconciliation. Sinners are reconciled with the Church and through this they are reconciled with God. The Church is the place where God is truly worshipped and the Holy Spirit is certainly present. Consequently it is fitting that grace should come to us through the Church. Through the sacrament of reconciliation those who have sinned grievously are restored to their full share in the Church's worship and in this way to communion with God.

Sin and community

Sin is an offence against God. It weakens or destroys the relationship between ourselves and God. Sin can also be an offence against our neighbour, when we sin against the Christ in everyman (*Mt 25:31*ff). As a result sin can not only impair the harmony that should exist within the individual himself, but it can also lead to a breakdown in the relationship between people (*ID 2*). Today more stress is being laid on this last point, as men become more and more conscious of the social aspects of sin and forgiveness. There are the sins which we as individuals commit against those around us and against society at large. There are also communal sins, that is to say sins of the various communities and social groupings to which we belong. For instance, there is the guilt we share in, through yielding to our social, national or even religious prejudices. Finally there is the teaching of the Vatican Council that by our sin we wound the Church of God (*LG 11*).

The body of Christ

The basic explanation of this place of the community and of the Church in our understanding of sin and forgiveness is the Christian mystery of the body of Christ. "Through a secret and

loving mystery of God's will men are joined together by a
supernatural bond in such a way that the sin of one injures the
others and the holiness of one benefits the others" (*ID 4*). We
are all one body, members one of the other (*Rom 12:20*f). By
our sins we take from the life of the whole body. By the
sacrament of Penance we are reincorporated or incorporated
more deeply into the full life of the body, and it is in this body
that we find union with Christ and reconciliation with God.

A sacrament of conversion

With the term "reconciliation" the New Testament underlines
how the sinner's return to God begins in a movement of divine
mercy and is entirely a work of grace (*Rom 5:10*f; *2 Cor 5:18*;
Eph 2:16). But reconciliation is a two-way process. The full
working out of this grace depends also on the sinner and on his
cooperation with the help God gives him. The reality we bring
to this sacrament is not only the sorrow in our hearts but also
our struggle with our own sinfulness and with the harm it is
doing to ourselves and to others. The sacrament should be
regarded as a special moment within a whole process of
conversion, which is both internal and external, individual and
social (*SC 109-110, Paen.*). We need external penance to
purify ourselves from our attachment to sin (*Paen. 11*). We
need social penance, if we are to make good the social values
which sin has lessened or destroyed; furthermore, we are called
to make reparation for others' sins as well as for our own
(*ID 3,5*). This entire struggle for conversion is the reality which
we bring to the sacrament, that it may be incorporated there
more deeply into the mystery of Christ's atonement (*Paen. 1*).

A sacrament of faith

Indeed there is a sense in which the active role of the
worshipper conditions the fruitfulness of every sacrament. All
the sacraments are sacraments of a living faith. From this the
Vatican Council derives the need for a more vital liturgy in each
sacrament, so that the worshipper's faith may be aroused,

involved and nourished by the very way the sacrament takes place (*SC 59*). In line with this the Council asks for a new liturgy of Penance also (*SC 72*). A mechanical and impersonal approach would be the opposite of what the Council has in mind. The sacrament must not be just administered but *celebrated*, and the very manner of celebration should bring out the various aspects of the sacrament which we have been stressing: that through Christ we can achieve victory over sin; that reconciliation implies reconciliation with the community; that the sacrament gives the Holy Spirit.

The word of God

One of the principal means which the Council points to for a deepening of faith in the sacrament is the word of God. "Faith", it says, "is born of the word and nourished by the word" (*PO 4*). The *Ordo Paenitentiae* also lays special emphasis on the celebration of the word, whether it is combined with a celebration of the sacrament or not (*OP 25; 36f*). A greater use of scripture is recommended even in the context of individual confession (*OP 17*). The ritual has many suggestions to offer of appropriate passages from the prophets and apostles (*OP 67ff*). Use might also be made of penitential and thanksgiving psalms.

Forms of celebration

As a result of this expansion of our penitential practice, the new ritual contains no less than four different forms of celebration:
Individual celebration of the sacrament;
Communal celebration with communal absolution;
Communal celebration with individual confession and absolution;
A scripture service on a penitential theme.

As is clear from these headings themselves, all but the last kind of celebration contain the sacrament. This last kind is recommended as a preparation, whether immediate or remote, for the reception of the sacrament (*OP 37*). For suggestions as to the manner and conditions of all the above kinds of celebration, the *Ordo Paenitentiae* should be consulted.

Penitence

As we have seen, the penitential process goes beyond the sacrament itself. Indeed devotion to this sacrament will develop only where the *virtue* of penance is understood and fostered. The sacrament implies a context in which penance is accepted as a constant aspect of Christian life. The new liturgy brings home to us how, even if we cannot bring people to the sacrament, we must still bring them to do penance and to take part in penitential worship, such as penance services or the Lenten Masses. Today it will be necessary to make clear that the relaxation of laws of fasting has not done away with the need to do penance but has only reduced the juridical determination of its forms. "By divine law," says Paul VI, "all the faithful are required to do penance" (*Paen. 3*). In particular the Church is anxious that Lent continue as a time of penance in preparation for the paschal mystery (*SC 110*). The faithful are still urged to honour the ancient custom of recalling our Lord's passion each Friday with some *voluntary* act of self-denial (Bishops of Ireland *Furrow* 1970, 533f).

INDIVIDUAL CONFESSION

One of the principal aims of the new ritual of penance is to ensure that the sacrament be celebrated in a personal and prayerful manner. A purely routine recital of sins and automatic dispensing of absolution are to be avoided as much as possible. The confessor's ideal should be to bring before the penitent sinner the image of the forgiving Christ (*OP 10c*). Attention should be paid to the following points in particular.

Dialogue

In the new ritual the entire sacrament is understood as taking place in a personal dialogue between priest and penitent. At the beginning the priest should welcome the penitent and, if necessary, put him at his ease. The use of the vernacular throughout makes it possible for each to listen to the other, even when the prayers are being said. Confessors might try to have something personal to say to each pentient in keeping with his state or the liturgy of the season. Absolution should not be given while the penitent is still saying his act of contrition, but in such a way that the penitent can hear it and understand it.

Scripture

In order to nourish the faith of the penitent as he celebrates the sacrament with the priest, use should be made of the scriptures, whenever the occasion allows (*OP 17*). Suggestions for appropriate passages will be found in the *Ordo Paenitentiae*, 67ff. Sometimes priest and penitent can alternate in reciting verses of the psalms, e.g. *Ps 31; 50; 129*. It will greatly help in the introduction of these practices if they are first explained to the people generally. It is suggested that confessors might commit a few suitable passages of scripture to memory (*OP 43*). Copies of the Bible or of a book containing appropriate passages of scripture might be left on the seats outside the confessional.[1]

Examination of conscience

Frequently this practice has lacked reality for many people, often because it was based on a list of sins found in some prayer book or learned in childhood. Sometimes, too, excessive importance has been given to computing number and kind in the case of venial sin, where the Church does not require it. In this matter the confessor will often have to assist his penitents (*OP 18*). He should help them to discover what is the real issue in their lives between themselves and God and to make this the principal subject of their examination of conscience. Nor should they be content merely with external categories of sin. Motivation and attitudes should be examined also.

---

[1] A useful pamphlet for this purpose is V. J. Weisberger, *Penance*, The Liturgical Press, Collegeville, USA.

Community

The communal aspect of this sacrament and of Christian life generally must be kept before priest and penitent alike. We cannot speak of reconciliation with God except in a context of reconciliation with one another. We cannot be truly devoted to this sacrament without becoming ourselves forgiving persons, marked by the compassion of Christ and by consideration of his presence in those around us. Sometimes this can be made clearer through the kind of penance imposed by the confessor; for instance, some act of kindness in the home or some act of service in the parish. It is often helpful in the course of the sacrament if priest and penitent pray together. Sometimes, too, the confessor should pray over his penitent as a sign of the whole community on whose prayers and merits he depends.

Penances

The penance imposed in confession is an act of reparation. It is a token of our union with the great act of atonement for our sins which was offered by Christ on the cross. It also carries with it, in virtue of the sacrament, a special grace of healing (*OP 8*). In particular it is a sign of our sincerity in our desire to change our lives and to be purified by the grace of Christ from our attachment to sin. Consequently penances should be related to the actual condition of the penitent and to the nature of the sin he has confessed, e.g. acts of kindness for failures in charity, acts of worship for faults of pride, self-denial for sins of sensuality.

Direction

Spiritual direction, as an aspect of the ministry of the word, can be an appropriate part of this sacrament. The confessor is not simply a dispenser of absolution. Nor should he be content merely with the correction of faults. Part of his task is to enkindle a deeper love of God in his penitents and to lead them to a more personal prayer and to a greater personal responsibility before God. He is also the guide of their repentance, directing and encouraging them beyond the penance imposed in the sacrament towards more voluntary mortification in their lives. A self-imposed act of penance after each fall is especially to be recommended as a means of dealing with the more serious habits of sin.

Confessions of devotion

Devotional confession of venial sin is recommended by the new ritual of penance. "Those who experience their weakness every day by falling into venial sin can draw strength from a repeated celebration of the sacrament, so that they may come to the full freedom of the sons of God" (OP 7). For such sins there are also other ways of forgiveness, but to submit them to the power of the keys in this sacrament expresses two things in particular. Firstly, it manifests the fact that we cannot grow in the life of God by our own powers alone. Secondly it is an acknowledgement of the ecclesial aspect of sin and forgiveness, namely that the Church is wounded by our sin and that the Church is our way to forgiveness.

Frequency

How often a person should go to confession is something that is best decided as a matter between priest and penitent. This sacrament is especially for the person who is struggling with sin and with the harm it is doing to himself and to others. Where this struggle is a reality in a person's life, he has grounds for coming regularly to confession. On the other hand, we should not expect that recourse to the sacrament will be indicated by a felt need on each occasion. To come to grips with the reality of sin in one's life is a grace into which one grows only gradually over a period of regular recourse to the sacrament. For a person making serious efforts to lead a spiritual life one might say that the interval between confessions should not be so brief that the sacrament becomes a routine, and it should not be so protracted as to become an expression of self-sufficiency and of forgetfulness of our need of grace.

Children and penance

The new ritual recommends that children be educated from an early age in the meaning of penance (*OP 37*). Particular care should be exercised that they be formed from the beginning in that more personal use of the sacrament which the new ritual has in mind throughout. Often it will be better not to bring large numbers of children at a time from the school to the church, but rather in smaller groups, e.g. class by class or year by year, so that confessors will have more time for each penitent. The new ritual makes special mention of penance services in the case of children (*OP 37*). Sometimes a brief service might be held to open or conclude a period of individual confessions. As regards First Confession, the ritual suggests that even prior to it the children might be made familiar with penance through celebrations of the word of God (*OP Appendix II 43*). According to a Declaration of the Sacred Congregation for the Discipline of the Sacraments and of the Sacred Congregation for the Clergy, confessions should precede the First Communion of the children (*AAS 65 [1973] 410; AAS 2 [1910] 577-583*).

COMMUNAL CELEBRATION OF PENANCE

As we have seen, three different kinds of communal celebration are envisaged in the new ritual. In all of them there is a celebration of the word of God but the relationship of each to sacramental absolution is different.

Communal celebration with communal absolution

This is not the normal way of celebrating the sacrament (*OP 31*). For the conditions governing such absolution, the new ritual should be consulted (*OP 31-34*).

Communal celebration with individual confession

This is a celebration of the word of God in the course of which facilities for individual confession are provided. It is useful where the proportion of confessors to penitents enables it to be carried out without undue delays. The aim should be that the whole celebration be seen as a unit.

A penitential Bible service

Such services are recommended by the new ritual as a way of fostering in the community the spirit of penance and of preparing people for a more fruitful use of the sacrament (*OP 37*). However, the ritual warns against confusing such services with the sacrament itself (*ibid.*).

Advantages

In any one of these three forms of communal celebration the following advantages may be found:

(a) They give an opportunity for bringing the penitential process into closer contact with the word of God, with all the benefits which the Vatican Council sees in such a contact (*OP 4; DV 21*).

(b) They permit a deeper formation of conscience than is possible during the normal Sunday homily or during individual confession. In particular such a formation should strive to make our people more aware of the communal aspects of sin:

1. Any refusal to do the will of God is an offence against the community, the Church, and takes from our communal vocation as members of the Church to live before God in holiness (*Mk 3:35; 1 Cor 12:26*).

2. Any offence against another individual or against society is an offence against Christ (*Mt 25:31ff*).

3. As well as our personal sins against others, there is also a guilt we share in through being members of communities which fail in their responsibilities. Group prejudice is a frequent source of such guilt.

(c) These celebrations clearly embody the role of the community in the forgiveness of sin and in our reconciliation with God. It is in forgiving one another that we ourselves are forgiven (*Mt 6:12; 18:35*). It is in the solidarity of a worshipping community, each one acknowledging a share in the common guilt, that we come to the true Christian humility which is the kernel of any lasting conversion.

Status of such celebrations
In presenting these various forms of celebration to the people, it will be important to explain how the Church's role here is to sustain and deepen the process of conversion of its members. These celebrations are no easy way out. There is no substitute for the penitential struggle with one's own sinfulness, but once this struggle is accepted, then it can be deepened and brought closer to God's grace by the Church's ministry, especially by the celebration of the sacrament.

With regard to services of penance where no absolution is given, it is helpful to recall the general teaching of the Church concerning the efficacy of contrition for the forgiveness of sin (*OP 37*). In such contrition, with its at least implicit desire for the sacrament, the effects of the sacrament can be anticipated. In so far as these services move the faithful to sentiments of contrition, they must be held to have some power for the forgiveness of our venial sins and they can represent an important step forward in the process of repentance for mortal sin.

Occasions
It is recommended that such celebrations be held several times a year. They are especially appropriate during Lent as part of our preparation for Easter and for going to confession at that time (*OP 13 Appendix II 5ff*). Advent, too, is recommended, for penitential services at that season will help to keep before the people the religious nature of Christmas (*OP Appendix II 20ff*). Such services will also be found useful at the time of retreats and missions and before the principal feasts. Finally it would be helpful if periods set aside for church confessions were to open and close with a penitential service, however brief, for the benefit of those who happen to be present.

5 Anointing and pastoral care of the sick

INTRODUCTION

Sickness is a reality of human life. Though we cannot explain it fully, we know from the words of Christ that it has meaning and value for our salvation. It is part of God's plan that we should struggle against sickness and seek the blessings of good health, so that we can fulfil our role in the world. Yet all the time we remember that in sickness we are called in a special way to share Christ's sufferings, who though he was without sin, took upon himself our weakness and suffered for us. Christ still suffers in his followers whenever they suffer. As sickness is a sign of man's sinful condition, so healing is a sign of Christ's victory over sin in which we can all participate. We must be prepared to fill up what is lacking in Christ's suffering for the salvation of the world. It is this "suffering and risen Christ" that we meet in the sacraments of the sick.

Unfortunately, sickness is too often the result of people's own neglect or over-indulgence, e.g. in eating, smoking, drinking. Here people can fail in Christian charity to themselves, as well as towards the other members of the community. Too many go recklessly on their way, damaging their health, and expecting the public to pay for the consequences, which are often extremely expensive. The apostolate of encouraging people to look after their own health, and to introduce some discipline and control into their way of life, needs to be encouraged.

The care of the sick is the responsibility of:
The Christian community. If one member of the Body of Christ

105

suffers, all the members suffer with him. The whole community, therefore, must show a special love and concern for the sick and express this concern in works of charity. When the Church cares for the sick, it serves Christ himself in the suffering members of his Mystical Body. It follows the example of the Lord Jesus who "went about doing good and healing". And since all the sacraments have a communal aspect, members of the community should be encouraged to participate in the sacraments of the sick.

The family and friends of the sick. They have a special share in the ministry of comfort. They should strengthen the sick with words of faith, praying with them and commending them to the Lord who suffered and is glorified. They should prudently dispose the sick for the reception of the sacraments at the proper time.

Priests. They should remember that "they are to care for the sick, visiting them and helping them by works of charity". They should stir up the faith of those present, strengthening their faith in Christ, especially when they celebrate the sacraments. They should comfort believers and raise the minds of others to God.

There are various stages in sickness, so for convenience, the *Rite of Anointing and Pastoral Care of the Sick* will be considered under three headings:

1. The care of the sick (cf. Chap. 1)
2. The care of those "dangerously ill" (cf. Chap. 2)
3. The care of the dying (cf. Chaps 3, 4, 5, 6).

THE CARE OF THE SICK

Visitation of the sick

All Christians should share in the care of Christ for the sick. More is required of them than just an enquiry after their health or a social call, good as these are. They should show their concern "by visiting them and comforting them in the Lord, offering them fraternal help in their need".

Priests especially and all who have the care of the sick should offer them words of faith and help them to realise that through their faith they are united with Christ's sufferings, and that with prayer they can sanctify their sickness and draw strength to bear their sufferings.

For the priest, visitation of the sick is a fundamental pastoral office. He should never allow it to degenerate into a mechanical routine. Any impression of haste is out of place. It is the *special task of the priest* to lead the sick step by step to the sacraments of Penance and the Eucharist and in particular to the sacraments of anointing and viaticum at the appropriate time.

The priest should always be ready to pray with the sick. Such prayer should draw primarily on the scriptures, "by meditating on those parts which speak of the mystery of human suffering in Christ and in his works, or by using prayers drawn from the psalms and other texts". Though no order for prayer with the sick is given — the condition of the sick varies so much — the following is suggested:

Scriptural reading(s)
Prayer drawn from psalms, or other prayers or litanies
Blessing
Laying on of hands (if circumstances indicate) — a gesture that continues the healing action of Christ.

As far as possible the priest should choose the readings, etc. in consultation with the sick person and those present. The priest, obviously, must lead in the ministry of the sick. If he takes this responsibility seriously, he will have his own collection of readings and prayers and make them available to lay people who are called on, from time to time, to carry out this service.

Communion of the sick

"Pastors of souls will take every care to make it possible for the sick and the aged to receive the Eucharist frequently, even if they are not gravely ill or in danger of death. In fact, if possible, this could be done every day, and should be done in Paschal time especially. Communion may be taken to these people any time of the day" (*EM 40*). Those who care for the sick may always receive communion with them.

Fasting
The *infirm* may take non-alcoholic liquids and liquid and solid medicines *without time limit* before Holy Communion. The period of eucharistic fast from *food and alcoholic drink* is reduced to about one quarter of an hour for the following persons:
(a) the infirm in hospital or at home, even though not confined to bed;
(b) the aged, whether detained by age at home, or living in a home for the aged;
(c) infirm or aged priests, whether they are about to celebrate Mass or receive communion;
(d) persons tending the sick or aged, and relatives who want to communicate with them, whenever they cannot observe the hour's fasting without inconvenience.

Requirements
Table covered with a linen cloth upon which the Sacrament is to be placed. If customary, a vessel of holy water and a sprinkler or small branch should be provided, as well as candles.

A vessel of water for the priest to rinse his hands (if necessary), or for the use of the sick person. The use of a crucifix, flowers, etc. is encouraged. In bringing communion outside the church, the sacred species should be carried in a pyx or other small closed container; the attire of the minister and the manner of carrying the Eucharist should be in keeping with the reverence due to the Sacrament, and appropriate to local circumstances.

Two forms are given for the communion of the sick:
1. The ordinary rite

2. The short rite

The ordinary rite
This is made up of:
Greeting (choice given);
Sprinkling the sick person and room (optional);
Penitential rite (three forms given) or sacramental confession;
Reading from scripture by one of those present or by priest. It
is important to make use of the selection given. The priest may
briefly explain the text;
"Our Father";
Communion;
Silence;
Concluding Prayer (choice given);
Blessing — with pyx if any of the sacrament remains, or by
using one of the blessings given. The priest might spend some
time afterwards praying with the sick person, using appropriate
prayers, short readings, etc.

The practice of having the priest met at the door by one of
those present carrying a lighted candle is to be encouraged.

The short rite
When communion is given in different rooms of the same
building (such as a hospital), the short rite is used.
The priest hears the confessions of the sick at a convenient time
beforehand.
The Rite of Communion is as follows:
Opening antiphon — said in the chapel or the first room. The
priest is escorted by a person carrying a candle.
"This is the Lamb of God" — to all the sick in the same room
or to each individually.
"Lord, I am not worthy" — by each communicant.
Concluding prayer — choice given.
Blessing omitted.

Elements from the ordinary rite may be added to this short
rite. "In case of necessity, depending on the judgment of the

bishop, it is permitted to give the Eucharist under the species of wine alone, to those who are unable to receive it under the species of bread. In this case it is permissible, with the consent of the local Ordinary, to celebrate in the house of the sick person" (*EM 41*).

Sunday and the sick

The whole parish is concerned for the brethren who are sick, and so the sick are remembered by their community at the Sunday Eucharist. Sunday is *the* day of the Christian assembly, and it is very appropriate that the sick, who are prevented from attending this celebration, should be nourished by the Eucharist on this day. Thus "they will feel themselves united to this community and sustained by the love of their brethren". As many priests would not be able to bring communion to the sick on a Sunday, communion could be brought by a deacon or an acolyte (where these are available), or by another of the faithful appointed by the bishop to distribute the Eucharist to the faithful.

Mass in the home of the sick

With the development of group Masses in recent times, Mass in homes is a more frequent occurrence. In such a situation Mass in the home of the sick would obviously commend itself. It is envisaged when communion is given under the species of wine alone and when it is given as Viaticum, but it should not be confined to these cases. Mass in their homes would link the sick with the liturgical community from which they are cut off through illness. The same applies to Mass in hospital wards or adjacent halls, which is so highly desirable, especially for long-stay or very infirm patients.

A special Mass "for the sick" is to be found in the Missal.

This Mass might usefully be celebrated occasionally during the year for all those unable to come to the church. This would be a recognition and expression of the part the sufferings of the sick can play in the life of the parish. It could also serve to remind others not to lose sight of the essential or higher things.

THE CARE OF THOSE WHO ARE DANGEROUSLY ILL

A distinction is made, in the new *Order for the Care of the Sick,* between those who are "dangerously ill" (*periculose aegrotant*), and those who are dying. What emerges clearly is that anointing is the sacrament for those who are seriously ill, whereas Viaticum is the sacrament of the dying. Even when it is administered to the dying, anointing is a sacrament of sickness, not of death, though it will, of course, have an important role to play at such a critical time in a person's life. Here we deal with the "seriously ill" — the care of the dying is dealt with below.

Extreme Unction, we are told, is more fittingly called the *Anointing of the Sick.* The change of name could help to change the popular attitude towards this sacrament, but a *mere* change of name will not be sufficient. Proper instruction and catechesis will be necessary if the people are to be led to a fuller understanding of the significance of the sacrament. Much useful material for instruction will be found in the Introduction to the new rites, as well as, of course, in the new rites themselves. Here we find the Church's understanding of the sacrament, which she sees as prolonging "the concern which the Lord himself showed for the bodily and spiritual care of the sick, and which he asked his followers to show also". "Christ came to save the 'whole man'", and so the sacrament of healing is directed to the whole man — to the healing of the whole person, (cf. *Introduction, 5*). Through the anointing of the sick the Church commends the sick to the suffering and glorified Lord. She asks that he may lighten their suffering and save them. The effect of the sacrament is summarised in section 6 of the *Introduction*: "The sacrament provides the sick person with the grace of the Holy Spirit by which the whole man is brought to health, trust in God is encouraged, and strength is given to resist the temptations of the Evil One and anxiety about death. Thus the sick person is able, not only to bear his suffering bravely, but also to fight against it. A return to physical health may even follow the reception of this sacrament if it would be beneficial to the sick person's salvation. If necessary, the sacrament also provides the sick person with the forgiveness of sins and the completion of Christian penance." Serious illness is a crisis in the life of a Christian. The sacrament of anointing brings him the help of Christ and his Church, enabling him to live his Christian life fully despite the special difficulty of sickness.

Use of oil

The oil to be used in the sacrament is olive oil, or if this is unobtainable, or difficult to obtain, any other plant oil. For convenience it should be soaked in cotton, and kept in a vessel that is clean and worthy. The priest should make sure that the oil remains fit for use, and so, if necessary, should obtain fresh oil from time to time. If the oil has to be disposed of, it should be absorbed in cotton wool and burned.

Symbolism of oil

The words of blessing express clearly the significance of the oil used in this sacrament: "oil intended to ease the sufferings of your people". Oil soothes and heals. Oil blessed for the sick is a sign of the Messiah, the Anointed of God. Those who are anointed with this oil receive the healing, saving power of the Messiah.

Blessing of oil

Ordinarily, the blessing of oil is reserved to the bishop, who blesses it during the Chrism Mass on Holy Thursday. But the law also permits the following to bless the oil of the sick:

(a) those whom the law equates with diocesan bishops;

(b) in the case of true necessity, any priest.

No examples are given of "true necessity". But, for example, if a priest, for some reason, either hasn't got any oil, or hasn't it with him, when called to anoint someone, and there is no time to get some, obviously he could bless oil. What is important is that the sick person be anointed. The priest himself, in any situation, may judge whether there is "true necessity". (However, if a priest in this country is in a position to bring unblessed oil with him, it is scarcely likely that he could not bring blessed oil).

If a priest is to bless the oil during the rite, he may bring unblessed oil with him, or it may be supplied by the family of the sick person.

If the oil is already blessed the priest says a prayer of thanksgiving over it (as he does over the baptismal water in Paschal time), or in place of it he may give an instruction.

Who may be anointed?

The requisite condition for receiving the sacrament of anointing is "serious illness" — not "danger of death". The sacrament is meant to be a *healing* of the sick (in the fuller sense of nos. 5, 6 of the *Introduction*, and not in the restricted sense of physical healing). And so "there should be special care and concern that those who are dangerously ill due to sickness or old age, receive this sacrament". The phrase used *periculose aegrotantes*, is taken from the *Praenotanda* of the Ritual of 1614, and in its history has been variously interpreted. A number of authors make no distinction between "dangerous illness" and "serious illness". The English "dangerously ill" is stronger than the Latin "periculose aegrotantes". It carries a nuance that the Latin does not — linking "danger" with "death". It would seem, then, that "serious illness" would better convey the meaning. The Introduction to the new rite, and the rite itself suggest that the phrase *periculose aegrotantes* should be widely interpreted. The *Constitution on the Liturgy*, 73, says that "as soon as any one of the faithful *begins* to be in danger of death from sickness or old age the fitting time for him to receive this sacrament has *certainly already arrived*". A person, then, who is seriously ill but not necessarily in danger of death may be anointed. There is no need for scruples. A prudent judgment by the priest or the patient himself about the seriousness of the illness is sufficient, though, if necessary, a doctor may be consulted. It should *not* be left to the doctor to suggest anointing. In public and private catechesis the faithful should be encouraged to ask for the anointing themselves.

Anointing is not a magic remedy. A person should as far as possible be able to take part in the celebration consciously and actively, and so the sacrament should be celebrated in good time. It is misusing the sacrament to "put it off".

Old people may be anointed if they are in a weak condition, even though no dangerous illness is present. It is not a question of anointing people who have reached a certain age. It is not simply a question of years, but of the debility that goes with age, and this varies from person to person. Here especially there is need for instruction, as older people so often regard anointing as a preparation for death.

Children may be anointed if they have sufficient use of reason to be comforted by this sacrament. Many young children could have sufficient understanding to so benefit, if given suitable instruction.

Before surgery: A person should be anointed if a dangerous illness is the reason for the surgery. Sympathetic consideration should be given to a request for anointing from anyone undergoing surgery.

Unconscious persons — or those who have lost the use of reason — may be anointed "if as Christian believers they would have asked for it were they in control of their faculties".

The dead should not be anointed. The priest should pray for the dead person, asking that God forgive his sins and graciously receive him into his kingdom. If there is a reasonable doubt whether a person is dead, the priest may administer the sacrament conditionally. A rite is given for conditional anointing. Here there would not seem to be any change in the traditional practice. However, the fact that we are now *expressly* told not to anoint the dead, could, perhaps, be interpreted as a corrective to any tendency to anoint in almost any such circumstances.

Repeating the sacrament

The anointing may be repeated if the sick person recovers after anointing and falls ill again, or if in the course of the same illness the danger becomes more serious. However, while the principle of repetition is fairly wide, one should avoid any rigid system of repeating the sacrament. In the case of a prolonged illness or a terminal illness one should not automatically repeat the sacrament after a certain length of time (e.g. monthly). Each case should be judged in itself. If the sickness grows worse or if there is a noticeable deterioration in the condition of the sick person, one may repeat the sacrament. A request for anointing from the sick person himself would often be a good indication. In all these matters, what is required is an ordinary prudent judgment.

Ordinary rite of Anointing

Preparation

The priest should enquire about the condition of the sick person, to plan the celebration properly and to choose the readings and prayers. The choice will depend on the condition of the sick person. It is desirable that this preparation be made with the sick person or with his family. The work of preparing the sick for the celebration of the various rites will make demands on the priest, but he will always find religious and laity ready to help in this work. Whenever it is necessary, the priest should, if possible, hear the confession of the sick person before the celebration. Otherwise the sick person confesses during the introductory rite.

If the sick person is not confined to bed, he may receive the sacrament in the church or some other suitable place.

In hospitals

The priest should take into consideration the other sick people — whether they are able to take part in the celebration, whether they are very weak, or, if they are not Catholics, whether they might be offended. We must be sensitive to the wishes and the feelings of other people.

Some hospital chaplains complain that they are often left to anoint people who should have been anointed before they came into hospital. The priest who cares for the sick of his parish will anoint them in good time and will regard this as his special responsibility. As well as that there is the time and the privacy in the home that is often lacking in hospitals.

Preliminary rites

In the former rite the opening prayers were really a blessing of the house. There was no special mention of the patient. The new rite is more personal. It is directed to the sick person, calling for his participation and that of those present.

The blessing with holy water, which is optional, is a reminder of Baptism and of our redemption through the death and resurrection of Christ.

The opening address — and the prayer which may be substituted for it — highlights the fact that anointing is the sacrament of healing, and not specifically a preparation for death.

"These or similar words" — the circumstances must dictate the words used. It may sometimes be inappropriate to emphasise the aspect of physical healing.

The penitential rite is celebrated if there is no sacramental confession. A number of alternative rites are given, but it is desirable that the priest occasionally compose his own variations on the third rite, adapting it to the particular circumstances (cf. 41. Penitential rite may be part of the introductory rite or may take place after the reading from scripture).

Reading from scripture. A large selection of suitable scripture readings is given. Normally the reading should be brief. A short explanation of the text may be given.

The litany is more appropriate at this point, though it may be said after the anointing, or, according to circumstances, at some other point. The priest may adapt or shorten the text.

The third form of the litany would be particularly suitable when the sick person finds it difficult to concentrate.

The laying on of hands is a welcome restoration. The priest now lays his hands *on the head* of the sick person. It is no longer just an extending of the hands over him. This rite continues in time Christ's gesture of healing in the Gospel. It is a sign of Christ's power over evil and of his goodness and compassion.

The blessing of oil is done at this point, if the oil is to be blessed. The prayer of blessing gives us good insight into the effects of the sacrament — a healing of the whole person.

Anointing

The new formula of anointing expresses more clearly the effect of the sacrament. The sacrament "provides the sick person with the grace of the Holy Spirit by which the whole person is brought to health, trust in God is encouraged, and strength is given to resist the temptations of the Evil One and anxiety about death". The old formula of anointing suggested that the sacrament was directed primarily to the sinful condition of the sick person.

The actual anointing should take place when the family and members of the community can be present. The rite prays that the sick person may be restored to the community, and so the community should be represented and join in the celebration.

There are now only *two anointings* — on the forehead and on the hands. These anointings embrace all human activities — thoughts and actions. The first part of the formula is said while the forehead is anointed and the latter part while the hands are anointed. The oil should *not* be wiped off after anointing, because of its sign value.

In *case of necessity,* a single anointing on the forehead is sufficient, or, because of the particular condition of the sick person, on another more suitable part of the body. In either case the whole formula is said.

Prayer

The anointing is followed by a prayer. Happily there is a choice. Five prayers are given, adapted to the condition of the sick person, e.g. advanced age, person in great danger, in last agony, etc.

Concluding rite

The rite concludes with the Lord's Prayer and the blessing of the priest.

Communion

If the sick person is to receive communion he does so after the Lord's Prayer. This is celebrated according to the Rite of Communion of the Sick, as already described. (Communion as Viaticum is dealt with later.)

The priest should follow the structure of the rite in the celebration, while accommodating it to the place and people involved.

Two or more priests may take part in the anointing of a sick person. In this case one of them says the prayers and performs the anointings, saying the sacramental formula. The others may take various parts, e.g. introductory rites, readings, invocations or explanations. They may each lay hands on the sick person.

Communal celebration

The sacraments are celebrations of the Church and, ideally, should be celebrated in a community setting. The new rite makes provision for this, and such a celebration can give a deeper insight into the meaning and the significance of the anointing of the sick, and the role of the community in this ministry of comfort.

a] During Mass

The anointing of the sick may take place during Mass, when the condition of the sick person permits and especially when Holy

Communion is to be received.

The celebration should take place in the church or, with the consent of the Ordinary, in a suitable place in the home of the sick person or the hospital.

The care and concern of the community for the sick can best be expressed by the support and prayers of the community gathered for the celebration of the Eucharist.

Mass for the Sick is celebrated, except on the Sundays of Advent, Lent, Easter season, Solemnities, Ash Wednesday and the days of Holy Week, when Mass of the day is celebrated.

Readings are taken from those given in the Lectionary for the Mass, or from the rite of anointing, unless the priest believes that it would be better for the sick person and those present to choose other readings.

The anointing fits into the structure of the Mass and takes place after the homily. The homily itself should be brief and based on the scripture texts. It should speak of the meaning of illness in God's plan of salvation, and of the grace given by the sacrament of anointing.

The anointing begins with the *litany*, or, if the litany or general intercessions follow the anointing, with the *laying on of hands*. This is followed by the blessing of oil or the prayer of thanksgiving over the oil, and then the *anointing itself*. There follow the *general intercessions*, unless the litany has preceded the anointing, and then the *Prayer after Anointing*.

The Mass continues with the presentation of the gifts. The sick person and all present may receive communion under both kinds.

b] Several sick persons

Where more than one person is being anointed, everything is done once and for all, and the prayers are said in the plural, except, (1) that the priest lays hands on each one individually, and (2) he anoints each one individually using the appointed form.

Anointing in a large congregation

This rite may be used for pilgrimages and other large gatherings of a diocese, city, parish or society for the sick. It may also be used, on occasion, in hospitals.

Obviously, where many sick are to be anointed at the same time, careful preparation will be necessary. This preparation will involve the sick who are to receive the sacrament, any other sick person who may be present, and also those who are in good health.

The full participation of all present should be encouraged by the use of appropriate songs, to foster common prayer and to express the Easter joy proper to this sacrament.

The rite should take place in a church or in some suitable place where the sick and others can easily gather. Such a communal celebration could be especially valuable in a home or hospital for the aged, where sometimes the sick feel "cut off" from the Church. It could give the sick and the aged a sense of "belonging" and be very instructive for all present, showing the part that sickness can play in the life of a parish or community.

During Mass

Reception of the sick takes place at the beginning of Mass after the greeting and the introductory words; the rest of the ceremony is that already described for anointing during Mass.

Outside Mass

The order outside Mass is:

Reception of the sick — the priest greets the sick and in his approach shows Christ's concern for human illness.

Penitential rite (if desired).

Scripture readings — one or more readings from the Lectionary for the sick or other more suitable readings.

Homily — which may be followed by a brief period of silence for reflection.

Litany/Laying on of hands.

Anointing — during which suitable songs may be sung, but only after the prayer of anointing has been heard at least once by those present.
General intercessions.
Prayer after anointing.
The Lord's Prayer — which may be sung by all.
Blessing; dismissal; appropriate song.

Several priests
When there are several priests present, each one lays hands on some of the sick and anoints them, using the sacramental formula. The principal celebrant recites the prayers.

The anointing: a sacrament of faith
The sacrament of anointing is not a magical remedy — it is a sacrament of faith. It demands faith in the one who administers it, and particularly in the one who receives it. "The sick man will be saved by his faith and the faith of the Church which looks back to the death and resurrection of Christ, the source of the sacrament's power ... and looks ahead to the future kingdom which is pledged in the sacraments."

It will, then, be the responsibility of the priest to look to his own faith and prayer life, and to stir up the faith of those present, especially the sick. He will do this above all through the proclamation of God's word in the readings and the homily, and through a careful and devout celebration of the rites themselves.

THE CARE OF THE DYING

Viaticum
Anointing is the sacrament of the sick. Viaticum is the sacrament of those who are facing death — of those who are dying of sickness, or are in danger of death from whatever cause. It is the sacrament of "our passage to the Father". Viaticum is the last sacrament before the journey through death

into life. "When the Christian, in his passage from this life, is strengthened by the Body and Blood of Christ, he has the pledge of the resurrection which the Lord promised: 'He who feeds on my flesh and drinks my blood has life eternal, and I will raise him up on the last day'. (*John 6:54*)." (*26*).

The idea of "passage with Christ to the Father" is part of every communion, but it is underlined in a special way and is celebrated in a special way in viaticum. The sick person, in receiving viaticum, accepts death and has the assurance that he is not alone in dying, for he is united to Christ in his dying and rising.

However, while we speak of viaticum as the "last sacrament" we must be careful not to identify it *necessarily* with the last communion that the sick person receives. Because the faithful should receive viaticum while still in full possession of their faculties, it will often happen that they will receive further communions even after they have received viaticum. Having celebrated one aspect of the Eucharist — "passage with Christ to the Father" — *solemnly* in viaticum, one would not repeat it on subsequent visits during the same danger of death, but give communion in the normal way for the sick. These communions can be seen as confirming or renewing the acceptance of death itself and belief in the resurrection that is expressed in receiving viaticum.

All baptised Christians who can receive communion and are in danger of death *are bound to receive viaticum*. Priests, therefore, must take every care to ensure that those who are in danger of death receive the Body and Blood of Christ in viaticum.

It is desirable that during the celebration of viaticum the sick person *should renew the faith he professed in Baptism*. Our "dying with Christ" begun in Baptism, is completed in our acceptance of death, in union with Christ, in viaticum.

For an effective celebration of viaticum, it is important that preparation should be given to the sick person, to his family and to those who take care of him.

Viaticum may be given during Mass or outside Mass — preferably during Mass.

During Mass

When possible, viaticum should be received during Mass (a) so that the sick person may receive communion under both kinds, and (b) because communion received as viaticum is a special sign of participation in the death of Christ and his passage to the Father — the mystery that is celebrated in the Eucharist.

Mass of the Holy Eucharist or *Mass of Viaticum* (white vestments) is celebrated except on Sundays of Advent, Lent, Easter season, on Solemnities, Ash Wednesday and days of Holy Week, when the Mass of the day is celebrated.

Mass is celebrated in the usual way, but the following should be noted:

A short homily should be given after the Gospel. It should take account of the condition of the sick person and explain the importance and meaning of viaticum to the sick person and to others present.

Baptismal profession of faith — if this takes place the priest should introduce it briefly at the conclusion of the homily. This renewal takes the place of the usual profession of faith in the Mass.

General intercessions — as usual, may be adapted to the particular celebration, or they may be omitted if the sick person has made the profession of faith and it appears that they will tire him too much.

Sign of peace — the priest and all present may give the sick person the sign of peace. This could reassure the sick person that he is not alone but has the love and support of the community.

In giving communion the priest uses the *form for viaticum*, a simpler and more expressive form than the old one.

The sick person and all present may receive communion under both forms. Those who are unable to receive under the species of bread may receive communion under the species of wine alone.

The priest may use the special form of blessing at the end of Mass, and may also add the form for the plenary indulgence for the dying.

Outside Mass

The order of viaticum outside Mass is as follows:

Greeting.

Sprinkling of sick person and room with holy water (optional).

Brief address or instruction — may be in one's own words.

Penitential rite — when sacramental confession is not part of the rite or if there are others to receive communion.

Plenary indulgence for the dying may be given at the conclusion of the sacrament or the penitential rite.

Scripture reading — a brief explanation of which is desirable.

Baptismal profession of faith.

Brief litany — if the condition of the sick person permits.

Lord's Prayer.

Viaticum.

Period of silent prayer followed by concluding prayer and blessing.

The priests and others present may give the sick person the sign of peace.

If no priest is available viaticum may be brought to the sick by:

(a) a deacon, who follows the prescribed rite in the ritual, or

(b) one of the faithful, man or woman, who has been appointed by the bishop to distribute the Eucharist to the faithful.

Ministers other than deacons use the rite they ordinarily follow for distributing communion, but with the special formula given in the rite of viaticum.

Continuous rite for those near death

This rite is provided for special cases. Up to this, it was more or less the normal practice, though the order was slightly different. But from now on it will not be normal procedure — the anointing will have taken place earlier. It will be for situations where sudden illness or some other cause unexpectedly places a person in danger of death. In such situations the sacrament of Penance, Anointing and the Eucharist as viaticum are given in a single service. This order restores viaticum to its original place — the last sacrament the Christian receives.

If the sick person is in *imminent danger of dying* he should be anointed immediately with a single anointing and then given viaticum.

In more urgent cases, *when death is near*, and there is not enough time to administer the three sacraments in the manner described, the person should be given viaticum immediately, without the anointing, so that in his passage from this life, he may be strengthened by the Body of Christ, the pledge of the resurrection. All the faithful are bound to receive this sacrament if they are in danger of death. Afterwards, if there is time, the sick person is to be anointed.

In either case the sick person should be given the opportunity to make a sacramental confession, which, of necessity, may be generic.

All this shows that in immediate danger of death it is viaticum that is important.

If because of his illness the sick person cannot receive communion, under the form of bread or wine, he should be anointed.

A special rite for anointing *without* viaticum is given.

Confirmation in danger of death

A short Rite of Confirmation for use in danger of death is provided in Chapter V of the new order. However, it is recommended that normally Confirmation in danger of death and anointing the sick should *not* be celebrated in a continuous rite, lest the two anointings cause confusion between the sacraments. If this is unavoidable, Confirmation is celebrated before the blessing of the oil of the sick. The imposition of hands which is part of the rite of anointing, is then omitted.

Rite of commendation of the dying

1. The word "commendation" comes from Christ's last word on the cross: "Father, into your hands I commend my spirit." The rite of commendation joins the death of the Christians with that of Christ.

2. The approach of death can cause fear and anxiety and a sense of isolation in the dying. They need to feel they are not alone. They need the care and support of the Christian community. They need faith and trust in God. The community can express its solidarity with them at this time especially by praying with them and commending them to God. Charity towards our neighbour who is dying urges us to express fellowship with him by praying with him for God's mercy and for confidence in Christ.

3. The rite is designed to arouse in the sick person faith and hope in the power of Christ's resurrection, and so overcome the fear of death. He is thus helped to accept death in imitation of Christ's death, and dies hoping for eternal life, which Christ won for us.

The rite of commendation is made up of short verses of scripture, scripture readings, litanies and prayers of various kinds.

These are used according to circumstances, and others may be added as the situation demands. The prayers do not form an integrated whole, and so the priest, or whoever is assisting the dying, will pick and choose, keeping in mind all the time that the sick tire easily. The prayers should be recited in a *slow*, *quiet voice* alternated with *periods of silence*. The sick must not be "oppressed" by too many words.

Other suitable prayers, ejaculations, and readings may be used.

It is also recommended that the dying person be signed with the Sign of the Cross, just as he was first signed at Baptism.

The readings and texts will offer consolation to those who are present, and will lead them to see death as a participation in the death of Christ and as leading to glory with him.

The *Litany of the Saints* is recommended if the condition of the sick person is such that he is unable to bear lengthy prayers. The litany is used when the Church wishes to ask special graces from God. Its use here emphasises the fact that Christian death is of concern to the whole Church.

Prayers of commendation are given for the moment when death seems to be near. And immediately after death the *Subvenite* should be said.

The priest or deacon should, whenever possible, assist the dying person and say the prayers of commendation and the prayer after death. Their presence shows that when a Christian dies, he does so in the fellowship of the Church. If the priest is unable to be present because of other serious pastoral responsibilities, he should instruct the laity to assist the dying, and make texts of the prayers and the readings available to them.

Conclusion

Like the other sacraments, the sacrament of the sick is the visible form of an invisible grace. The more intelligible the rites used, the more firmly and effectively they will enter the minds and lives of the faithful. A change of name, a change of rites is not sufficient. All who participate must try to understand their significance and the doctrines underlying them. Here the role of the priest is all important. He must suitably instruct people on the meaning of the rites for the sick. He must, in arranging the rite — while following the structure of the rite — accommodate it to the time, place and people involved. The needs of one sick person are not those of another, so he will take into account the wishes of the sick person and other members of the faithful. He should make use of the different options given and of the wide selection of texts provided in Chapter VII. He should not forget the duty of thanksgiving, and therefore, should encourage the sick who have regained their health to give thanks to God, e.g. by participating in a Mass of thanksgiving, or in some other appropriate way. Above all he must stir up the hope of those present and strengthen their faith in Christ who suffered and was glorified. It is only through faith that we meet the Christ who once exercised the ministry of healing in his visible humanity, and now exercises that same ministry in the sacrament of the sick.

6 Ordination to the Priesthood

Introduction

Ordinations should take place, normally, in the cathedral. The holding of the ceremony in the parish church is also of undoubted value, and can be a high point in the liturgical life of the parish. Many people can be involved in the preparation for and the celebration of the Rite of Ordination to the priesthood — the priests of the parish, altar servers, choir, youth clubs, parish organisations and, especially, the family of the ordinand.

Preparations for the ceremony

It is important that the ceremony be announced well in advance. The date and time should be arranged so that as many as possible of the community can be present. The Prayer of the Faithful on the Sundays preceding the ceremony might include a petition for the ordinand. If there is a diocesan director of vocations he might be invited to preach in the parish some time before the ceremony. Schools in the parish should also be informed about the function and this is an opportunity for priests and teachers to give the pupils some explanation of the new Rite of Ordination to Priesthood. It might be useful too, to make texts of the ceremony available in the church bookstall. An ordination also gives an opportunity to increase the musical repertoire of the congregation and parish choir.

Local organisations in the parish should also be invited to attend and participate in the ceremony, e.g. Boy Scouts, Girl Guides, and members of youth clubs. All should keep in mind that the visit of a bishop to a parish, particularly if it is the bishop of the diocese, should be an important occasion in the life of the local community (*SC 41*).

Preparation for an ordination ceremony involves team work between the parish clergy, choir, altar servers and the ordinand. An appropriate programme of music should be arranged.

Choir
The general principles already given on page 58 apply here. In addition to their usual role, the choir should always lead the congregation in chanting the litany and the hymn to the Holy Spirit during the investiture ceremony. Suitable motets could also be included at various points in the celebration.

Altar servers
For the ordination ceremony it is suggested that there be eight servers to assist the bishop — thurifer, incense-bearer, cross-bearer, two servers to carry candles flanking the cross, book-bearer, mitre and crozier-bearers. Rehearsals should be held with the servers before the ceremony.

Commentator
A commentator would be useful to introduce the rite before the function begins. If the congregation have texts of the ceremony the commentator's intrusion into the rite itself should be kept to an absolute minimum. During the ceremony the texts should be allowed to speak for themselves.

Responses of the ordinands should be audible and may need to be given through the microphone. However, if a number are being ordained it may suffice for one or two ordinands to be heard; otherwise repetition may give rise to monotony. Effective use of singing or music can be made at such moments.

Relatives of ordinands
Special places near the sanctuary should be reserved for the parents and family of the ordinands.

Ceremony
At the appointed time, the procession comes from the sacristy

and enters the church by the main door as follows: thurifer and incense-bearer, cross-bearer flanked by servers with lighted candles, book-bearer, other servers, clergy in choir dress, the ordinand vested as a deacon, concelebrating priests, the bishop flanked by a deacon (or two deacons) and the mitre and crozier-bearers. On arrival in the sanctuary all genuflect or bow and go to their appointed places.

After the incensation of the altar, the bishop begins the ordination Mass at the chair. The ceremony should be briefly introduced by the bishop after he greets the congregation.

The readings may be chosen from the Mass of the day and/or from the section on Holy Orders in the Lectionary.

After the reading of the gospel, the candidate is called by the deacon and presented to the bishop by the parish priest or other priest designated.

The homily by the bishop follows. The instruction given in the Rite of Ordination may be used or the bishop may use his own words. For the homily the candidate should be seated in the sanctuary facing the bishop.

Following the homily the examination of the candidate and the promise of obedience by the candidate takes place.

The next part of the ceremony is the Litany of the Saints and this is prefaced by an invitation to prayer by the ordaining bishop. The Litany may be recited or sung by a group of chanters. The names of other saints, e.g. patron of diocese or religious order or congregation, the titular of the church, the patron saint of the candidate, may be added in their proper place in the Litany.

Suitable petitions for the occasion may be inserted into the Litany. These petitions should be prepared and written out beforehand. Because of the Litany, with its petitions, the Prayer of the Faithful is omitted. The Litany concludes with the prayer by the bishop.

The laying on of hands

The laying on of hands (cf. p 45 under Confirmation), and the prayer of consecration which follows, is the most solemn part of the ordination ceremony. The bishop lays his hands on the head of the candidate in silence. Beginning with the concelebrants, all the priests present do likewise. Priests who are not concelebrating and wish to impose hands should be vested in soutane, surplice and stole. It is important to note that singing and organ music are out of place at this point in the ceremony. For the prayer of consecration, the priests should stand forming a corona around the ordaining bishop.

Investiture
This is done by one of the priests present. The stole is re-arranged and the newly ordained is vested in the chasuble. It is suggested that some priest designated by the candidate do this.

Anointing with chrism
When the newly ordained has been vested as a priest, he goes to the bishop who anoints his hands with the oil of chrism.

During the vesting and anointing the *Veni Creator* or other suitable hymn is sung. It is suggested that the singing of the hymn might be interrupted so that those present can hear the formula for anointing.

Presentation of gifts
After the anointing, the bishop and the candidate wash the oil from their hands. This is an opportunity for those taking part in the procession with the gifts to go to the place (preferably the end of the church) where the gifts are ready. It is suggested that the procession with the gifts take place at this point in the ceremony because the formula for presentation to the new priest underlines the fact that the gifts come from the people to be offered to God. The paten with the bread and the chalice with the wine and water are given by the deacon to the bishop, who presents them to the newly ordained. An appropriate hymn may be sung at this point.

Kiss of peace

The Ordination Rite concludes with the kiss of peace given by the bishop to the new priest. The newly ordained may also receive the kiss of peace from the other priests present — this symbolises a welcoming of the candidate into the priesthood.

Mass

The Mass resumes at the altar and the new priest takes the first place among the concelebrants.

The parents and immediate family of the new priest may receive Holy Communion under the species of bread and wine from the new priest. Those who have already received Holy Communion at an earlier Mass may receive again here.

7 Marriage

Doctrine

Marriage is:

a life-long covenant of love, involving total fidelity and unbreakable oneness;

ordained to the procreation and education of children;

a sign of Christ's loving union with his Church;

a path to holiness, in fact *the* path to holiness proper to married people;

an apostolate to the world.

This rich doctrine is enshrined in the rite of marriage. The rite emphasises:

the dignity of human love;

the enriching of human love which takes place through the sacrament;

the obligations of the couple towards each other and towards their children;

the grace of the sacrament, which helps the couple in the living out of their married life;

the role of the family as the domestic Church, in which the parents, by their word and example, should be the first preachers of the faith to their children.

Priests should bear this teaching in mind, both in their instruction of those preparing for marriage, and in their approach to the celebration of the sacrament.

Pastoral importance of marriage

The celebration of marriage is a valuable pastoral moment in the life of the whole Christian community. The priest can play a most important role in helping to make the occasion a veritable "hour of grace" for the couple, an event with profound spiritual repercussions in their lives.

The congregation tends to be particularly well-disposed and receptive on the occasion of marriage. For them, as for the bridal couple, the ceremony can be a moving religious experience. Hence the importance of careful preparation for the celebration.

Instruction of the couple

(a) In his discussions with the couple before marriage the priest should help them understand the Church's teaching on marriage as already outlined.

(b) He should strengthen and nourish their faith, for the sacrament presupposes and demands faith. He should encourage them to prepare spiritually for the sacrament through prayer and penance.

(c) He should familiarise them with the ritual of the sacrament, particularly the text. Copies of the rite should be made available.

(d) The couple should be encouraged to make their own choice of prayers and readings.

(e) As a help in their preparation for marriage the couple should be encouraged in good time to follow a pre-marriage course. Through such a course they learn to understand better what is involved in living together as husband and wife. They will also discover how to deepen their spiritual relationship with each other, and come to an appreciation of their responsibilities as married partners and parents.

(f) A rehearsal of the ceremony can be invaluable. It is the best preventative against nervousness.

(g) The reader should prepare for his function. He should be helped to understand the sacred text and to appreciate that his role in proclaiming God's word is a prophetic one. He should familiarise himself with the amplification system, and rehearse his readings in the church itself. Where appropriate, a relative might be asked to act as reader. Because of the reverence due to the sacred text, the reader should read from a lectionary, and not from a missalette or slip of paper.

Preparation of setting

(a) It is useful to provide:

Separate texts for bride and groom — this eliminates the necessity of having a chart or book passed between the couple, a gesture which can look ungainly.

a salver on which rings and coins can be placed beforehand — this eliminates the embarrassing fumbling which can occur when the best man is asked to produce these objects during the ceremony itself.

(b) In deference to the sacrament and in courtesy to those who have come in good time, especially if a public Mass is being celebrated, the couple themselves should arrive in time.

(c) The places for the couple should be so located as to facilitate maximum audibility and visibility, and the fullest participation by the congregation. Good participation is not possible, normally, if the couple have their backs to the congregation.

(d) No special honours should be paid to any particular couple whether in the course of the ceremonies, or by external display.

Celebration of the sacrament within Mass

The marriage ceremony is an occasion of great joy and happiness. It is fitting that the entire celebration should reflect this spirit as clearly as possible. All the means and resources available should be used to bring home to those present the greatness of the event taking place.

In large churches a sense of isolation and the likelihood of lack of participation by the congregation may possibly be overcome (a) if the group of guests is small, by moving them to seats behind the altar rails and surrounding the altar, but not in a manner that will impede the priest, (b) if the group is large (from 50 upwards) by allowing the bride and groom, witnesses and both sets of parents to be seated at the altar and moving those seats in the body of the church which will be occupied by the remaining guests, closer to the altar.

Alternatively, if a side chapel is available, and the couple wish to use it, it can because of its size lend a greater sense of intimacy and warmth.

The ceremony

1. *Music:* Music has always been regarded as an important element in the celebration of marriage. Sometimes it is treated as mere pleasant background material rather than as a direct element in the celebration. Therefore, an examination of musical possibilities, followed by a review of resources available, should help all concerned to approach the celebration in a more positive way.

To ensure a musical programme which corresponds to the requirements and abilities of all present, there should be adequate consultation in advance. The bride, groom, priest, organist, cantor/soloist and choirmaster should all be involved in this consultation.

The congregation should be encouraged to participate through song. This is in fact an ideal which should never be submerged in other more immediate or conventional solutions. The problem of preparing the congregational music could be overcome, for instance, by a rehearsal in the church or even in the homes of the bride and groom.

The soloist, if there is one, should be encouraged to contribute to the celebration in a fully liturgical way. Solo singing at weddings is much appreciated, but more important is the role of the soloist as cantor, alternating in song with the congregation. Solo music may be sung from the organ gallery, but the responsorial psalm and alleluia verse are ideally sung from the ambo.

It is recommended that soloists offer a worthwhile list of possible music rather than the one or two sentimental items which people have been constantly requesting up to now.

Sometimes solo items are requested which in no way reflect the profound Christian sacrament which is being celebrated. Sound judgment is required of all concerned. The dignity of the sacrament must always be kept in mind.

Choirs sometimes participate in the wedding ceremony, a fact very much determined by the time of the wedding and the availability of members. If there is a choir, the principles given on page 58 apply.

2. *Arrival of the bride and groom:* The priest, at a suitable place in the church, e.g. at the entrance to the church, or at the sanctuary, greets the bride and groom in a friendly way, showing that the Church shares their joy.

3. *Introductory greeting:* The greeting at the beginning of Mass should reflect the joy of the occasion. A word of welcome might appropriately be extended to visitors from other localities. The celebrant should show special consideration to those who are not of his faith, or who are lukewarm in the practice of the faith. He should show sensitiveness to the presence of such people throughout the entire celebration.

4. *The homily:* There is always to be a homily. The celebrant should speak of the mystery of Christian marriage, the dignity of married love, the grace of the sacrament, and the responsibilities of married people. He should keep in mind the circumstances of the particular marriage. The homily should not be a eulogy of the couple or their families.

5. The placing of the marriage celebration after the homily helps to bring out the connection between the "covenant of marriage" and the covenant between God and man which is renewed in the Eucharist.

6. The address and ensuing questions aim at eliciting from the couple a statement in the presence of the community, represented especially by the priest, of their understanding of marriage and their freedom to marry.

7. *Declaration of consent:* Through the declaration of consent the priest asks for and receives the consent of the couple, according to the requirements of the *Constitution on the Liturgy.*

With prior encouragement from the priest the couple could memorise the exchange of consent. The text should be made available to them some weeks in advance.

8. *"What God joins together . . ."* This declaration and prayer express the intervention of God who confirms the consent of the couple and enriches them with the grace of the sacrament.

9. *Blessing of rings:* The ring, as the formularies of blessing indicate, is a symbol of the fidelity of husband and wife and a reminder of their love.

10. The gold and silver bring out the role of husband as provider for his household.

11. It may be desirable to invite bride and groom to announce some of the intentions in the Prayer of the Faithful.

12. *Preparation of the gifts:* Ideally the couple should carry the gifts in the procession. The procession should be a short one; in that way an additional formal procession of bride and groom through the nave is avoided.

13. The proper preface of the nuptial Mass is rich in content. If it is used, the fourth eucharistic prayer may not be chosen. The Roman Canon, if used, offers a special *Hanc Igitur* formulary, rich in content.

14. At the words *Let us offer each other the sign of peace* the couple and all present show their peace and love for one another in an appropriate way. Having exchanged the sign of peace with each other the bride and groom might exchange it with the bride's family and, then, the groom's; then perhaps with the congregation.

15. The reception of Holy Communion by the bride, the groom and the faithful is of special importance. The bride and groom may receive from the chalice.

16. The nuptial blessing and the blessing at the end of Mass re-echo some of the main themes of the rite.

17. The signing of the civil register may take place following the prayer after communion. Having it at this point eliminates, for the congregation, the uneasiness and tedium of waiting. In this case the register is signed in the sanctuary.

18. The final blessing of the Mass now follows.

Marriage outside Mass

The marriage takes place within the context of a liturgy of the word. The foregoing directives apply *mutatis mutandis*.

8 Christian Burial

Death is not the end. The Christian sees in it the beginning of a new life. In the funeral rite the Church celebrates the paschal mystery: Christ's passing, the Christian's passing, from this world to the Father.

The purpose of the funeral rite is:

1. to commend the dead to God;
2. to support the Christian hope of the people;
3. to give witness to our faith in the future resurrection of the baptised with Christ.

Structure of the rite

The rite has three main divisions or "stations" corresponding to the important moments between the death of a person and the burial of the remains. The various prayers and ceremonies, including the celebration of the Eucharist, which are used in the carrying out of these stations are intended both as a supplication for the soul of the deceased and to console the mourners and strengthen their faith in the resurrection and the hope of eternal life.

First Station: In the home
Second Station: In the church
a] Reception of the body
b] Funeral Mass
c] Final commendation
Third Station: At the grave

Various elements of the rite

Of the various elements which make up the rite the *Introduction* underlines three in particular: readings, psalms and prayers (*Intro. 9-11*). Special emphasis should be given to the readings from scripture, since they "proclaim the paschal mystery, support the hope of reunion in the kingdom of God, teach respect for the dead, and encourage the witness of Christian living" (*9*). The psalms are used to express grief and to strengthen genuine hope. Priests are urged to try to help their people to understand and appreciate the use of the psalms in this context. In the prayers of the funeral rite the Christian community once again expresses its faith and intercedes for the deceased that they may enjoy eternal happiness with God. Mention is made of the special function of prayers at the funerals of children to console the parents in their particular sorrow and strengthen their faith.

In the celebration of the funeral rites Christians should bear in mind that grief is human. Grief, too, is Christian. The Lord himself grieved at the graveside. To attempt to repress legitimate grief, when one's emotions are leading one to grieve, is to stifle a natural healthy response to bereavement, which even from a psychological point of view can be ill-advised. An old saying goes:"To grieve is human. To hope is Christian." Grief, alongside Christian hope and confidence, has its place in the Christian response to death.

Ministry

"In funeral celebrations all who belong to the people of God should keep in mind their offices and ministry: the parents or relatives, those who take care of funerals, the Christian community as a whole, and finally the priest. As teacher of the faith and minister of consolation, the priest presides over the liturgical service and celebrates the Eucharist" (*14*).

Through prayerful, sensitive celebration the priest can

breathe spirit into the funeral celebration, clothing the naked ritual with a meaning and dignity which, without stifling legitimate grief, will support the hope of the bereaved and the congregation in the life to come.

"Priests and all others should remember that, when they commend the dead to God in the funeral liturgy, it is their duty to strengthen the hope of those present and to foster their faith in the paschal mystery and the resurrection of the dead. In this way the compassionate kindness of mother Church and the consolation of the faith may lighten the burden of believers without offending those who mourn" (*15*).

"In preparing and arranging funeral celebrations priests should consider the deceased and the circumstances of his life and death and be concerned also for the sorrow of the relatives and their Christian needs. Priests should be especially aware of persons, Catholic or non-Catholic, who seldom or never participate in the Eucharist or who seem to have lost their faith, but who assist at liturgical celebrations and hear the gospel on the occasion of funerals. Priests must remember that they are ministers of Christ's gospel to all men" (*16*).

The entire funeral rite, except of course the Mass, may be celebrated by a deacon. If a priest or deacon is unavailable the stations in the home and at the grave may and should be celebrated by a lay person.

The new rite makes no definite stipulations about the colour to be used at funerals beyond stating that it "should not be offensive to human sorrow but should express Christian hope enlightened by the paschal mystery" (*19*). In the choice of colours the feelings of the mourners and the individual circumstances should be taken into account.

Preparing the celebration

As with all the renewed rites published since Vatican II, the new funeral rite offers a large selection of texts. Priests are most strongly urged to make full use of all the possibilities, making judicious selection of texts according to the particular circumstances of each funeral. If at all possible and opportune they should consult the family in making these choices. Members of the family should be given the opportunity of taking part as fully as possible in the funeral celebration, for example by acting as readers and presenting the gifts at the funeral Mass. A discreet visit to the home of the family can serve a double purpose of both consoling the bereaved in their sorrow and helping them to derive strength and courage from a deeper appreciation of the meaning of the funeral celebration.

The individual rites

First Station: In the home of the deceased
This may take place in the home any time between the laying out and the removal of the body to the church. The rite is also appropriate for use in the mortuary chapel of a hospital just prior to the departure of the funeral for the church. If a priest or deacon is unable to be present, the prayers should be led by a lay person.

Second Station: In the church
a] *Reception of the funeral*
In this country the normal custom is to bring the body to the church some time before the funeral Mass is to be celebrated, usually the previous evening. Where convenient, the coffin should be placed before the altar.

The priest receives the funeral at the church door, sprinkling the body with holy water. The rite suggests that a responsory be said or sung as the procession moves into the church.

Before beginning the prayers, it is appropriate that the priest should say a few words of greeting, offering his sympathy to the relatives of the deceased.

The custom of placing Mass cards on the coffin is open to abuse and misunderstanding, and should not be encouraged. The new rite suggests that the gospel book or a Bible or cross might be placed on the coffin. It is strongly recommended that the paschal candle be placed at the head of the coffin as a symbol of the paschal mystery and a sign of Christian hope in the resurrection. This gesture is preferable to the former custom of placing brown mourning candles around the coffin. Its significance might be briefly explained at some point during the rite, for example during the "few words of greeting" mentioned above.

It is particularly recommended that there be some priest or priests available to hear confessions on the occasion of the reception of a funeral. Death comes unexpectedly and the relatives and friends of the deceased who may wish to receive Holy Communion at the funeral Mass might also wish to have confession. Death is also very often the occasion of a return to grace of those who may have allowed their faith to lapse for many years. Priests should be sensitive to the pastoral opportunities of occasions such as these.

If the body is brought to the church immediately before the funeral Mass, there is no special ceremony. The priest, vested for Mass, simply receives the funeral at the church door, sprinkling the body with holy water and offering his sympathy to the relatives. As the funeral procession moves up the church the entrance hymn or introit antiphon or suitable responsory may be sung or recited.

b] *The Mass*

A special effort should be made to allow the relatives of the deceased to take part as fully as possible in the planning and celebration of the Mass. Two readings may be used in addition to the gospel, in which case the first will be taken from the Old Testament.

The choice of music should be discussed. The music should be chosen with deference to the sensibilities of the mourners. It should express their faith and hope.

There should be a homily at the funeral Mass. Care must be taken that it does not become any kind of funeral eulogy; it should centre rather around the Christian understanding of death in the light of the resurrection.

Every encouragement and opportunity should be given to the family and relatives to share most fully in the Eucharist by receiving Holy Communion. As already mentioned, the availability of confession the previous evening can be most helpful in this respect.

When the funeral takes place immediately after Mass the blessing and dismissal are omitted. Immediately after the Prayer after Communion the priest begins the rite of commendation and farewell.

c] *Final commendation and farewell*

This rite takes the place of the former absolution and represents the single most important innovation in the new funeral rite. It has been drawn up to reflect the paschal understanding of death, and so has not got the heavy emphasis on judgment which characterised the former rite. "It is not to be understood as a purification of the dead — which is effected rather by the eucharistic sacrifice, but as the last farewell with which the Christian community honours one of its members before the body is buried. Although in death there is a certain separation, Christians who are members of Christ and are one in him, can never be really separated by death" (8).

The rite begins with an invitation to pray, after which there should be a definite pause for silent prayer. The priest then sprinkles the body with holy water and incenses it. The *Introduction* (8) reminds us that the sprinkling with holy water recalls the person's entrance into eternal life through Baptism, and the incensation honours the body of the deceased as a temple of the Holy Spirit.

The responsory follows. If it cannot be sung, it should be recited in a responsorial fashion and the faithful should be invited to join in the responses. The invocations "Lord, have mercy", etc. may be recited after the responsory; but they should not be followed by the Our Father, which has already been said during the Mass. The rite concludes with the final prayer and the singing or recitation of an antiphon.

The priest should lead the funeral procession out of the church and at the door he may sprinkle the body once again with holy water.

Third Station: At the grave
The main characteristic of the rite at the graveside is its brevity and simplicity. The actual burial is perhaps the most difficult moment for the relatives, and so should not be protracted longer than is necessary. Normally the grave will already have been blessed; if not it is blessed before the interment. After the prayer of commendation, if it is the custom, some earth may be scattered on the coffin; it should be remembered that this could be the cause of distress to the bereaved, and so should only be done where there is a genuine custom.

After the Prayer of the Faithful and the Our Father or concluding prayer, a prayer for the bereaved may be said, and the rite concluded with a decade of the Rosary, though it might be more prudent to omit this if the weather is very bad or the relatives particularly distressed.

Vigil for the Deceased

The vigil is a further innovation in the new funeral rite. It is a service of the word which may be celebrated either in the home of the deceased or in the church. It is offered as an alternative to the recitation of the Office of the Dead. Its use is always optional. If it is celebrated in the church, the most appropriate time is some time in the evening before the funeral Mass; it may in fact be integrated with the reception of the funeral.

Since it is in fact a liturgy of the word, the vigil should never immediately precede the celebration of the funeral Mass, as this would involve duplication.

Funerals of children

One of the most difficult tasks in the pastoral ministry is

comforting the parents of a child that has died. The new rite offers much assistance in this in the texts for the funerals of children. Rather than concentrating solely on the fact that these children share immediately in eternal happiness, the texts offer hope and consolation to the parents in their sorrow and encourage them to strengthen their faith.

Priests should be particularly sensitive to the needs of parents on such occasions and special care should be taken to choose, both for the Mass and for the funeral rite, the texts most suited to the particular circumstances. The liturgical colour used should always be white.

A feature of the new rite is that it offers texts to be used at the funerals of children who die before Baptism. This rite can be most consoling to the bereaved parents of such a child. Care must be taken however not to weaken the doctrine of the necessity of Baptism.

9 Ministries of Lector and Acolyte

Two ministries in the celebration of the liturgy may be committed to lay Christians: the ministry of lector and the ministry of acolyte.

Lector
It is the lector's responsibility:
to proclaim the word of God in the liturgical assembly;
to instruct children and adults in the faith, and prepare them for worthy reception of the sacraments;
to announce the Gospel to those who do not already know it.
(cf. *Rite of Institution of Lectors.*)

> "Accordingly it will be his task to read the lessons from the scripture (but not the Gospel at Mass and at other sacred functions); when there is no psalmist he will recite the psalm between the readings; he will announce the intentions at the prayer of the faithful when the deacon or cantor is not present; he will direct the singing and the participation of the faithful; he is to instruct the faithful in the worthy reception of the sacraments. He may also when necessary prepare the faithful who are temporarily appointed to read the scriptures in liturgical celebrations. He should meditate assiduously on the sacred scriptures so that he may more fittingly and perfectly fulfil these functions." — Pope Paul VI in *Ministeria Quaedam,* 15 August 1972.

Acolyte
It is the acolyte's responsibility:

to assist the priests and deacons at the Eucharist;
to give Holy Communion, as an auxiliary minister, to the
faithful at the liturgy and to the sick.
(cf. *Rite of Institution of Acolytes.*)

"An acolyte is appointed to assist the deacon and to
minister to the priest. It is his duty therefore to attend to
the service of the altar, to assist the deacon and the priest in
liturgical celebrations, especially in the celebration of
Mass. It also falls to him to distribute Holy Communion,
as an extraordinary minister, whenever ministers listed in
Canon 845 of the code of canon law are not present, or are
themselves unable to distribute Holy Communion when
the number of communicants would otherwise be
considerable enough to prolong the celebration of Mass
unduly. It is also permissible to entrust to him, in similar
extraordinary circumstances, the task of exposing the
blessed Sacrament for the veneration of the faithful and of
replacing it subsequently. He may not, however, bless the
people. He may also as the need arises instruct those of the
faithful who are temporarily appointed to assist the priest
and deacon by carrying the missal, the cross or the candles
or by performing other similar duties in liturgical
celebration. He will perform these duties more worthily if
he participates in the holy Eucharist with ever-increasing
fervour, is nourished by it and deepens his understanding
of it" — *Ministeria Quaedam.*

Qualifications required for ministry of lector or acolyte

The offices of lector and acolyte are reserved to men, in keeping
with the venerable tradition of the Church. Before a person can
be admitted to these ministries he must fulfil the following
conditions:

(a) He must freely draw up and present a signed petition to
the ordinary who has the right of acceptance. The ordinary
is the bishop or, in the case of clerical institutes of
perfection, the major superior.

(b) He must have attained the age and must possess the qualities determined by the episcopal conference.

(c) He must have the firm intention of serving God and the Christian people — *Ministeria Quaedam*.

Conferring of ministries

The ministeries are conferred by the Ordinary (the bishop, or in clerical institutes of perfection, the major superior).

10 Function of Deacon

The demands of the liturgy and the need to give better service to our people call for the use of deacons, where they are available.

With regard to deacons the following should be especially kept in mind:

(a) "In the lower grade of the hierarchy are deacons, on whom hands are laid 'not for the priesthood, but for the ministry' *(Constitutions of the Church of Egypt, III, 2)*.

(b) Strengthened by sacramental grace they serve the people of God in the *diaconia* of liturgy, word and charity, in communion with the bishop and his *presbyterium*" (cf. *LG 29*).

Functions of deacon

It pertains to the office of a deacon, in so far as it may be assigned to him by the competent authority:

to administer Baptism solemnly;

to be the custodian and distributor of the Eucharist;

to assist at and to bless marriages;

to bring Viaticum to the dying;

to read the sacred scripture to the faithful;

to instruct and exhort the people;

to preside over the worship and prayer of the faithful;

to administer sacramentals;

to officiate at funeral and burial services (*LG 29*).

11 Music in the liturgy

Purpose of Music

The purpose of music in the liturgy is to give worship a "more noble form" (*MS 5*). The Church sees music not as an optional extra but as a "necessary or integral" part of her liturgy (*SC 112*). The role of music in liturgy is that of a servant. It has a "ministerial function" (*SC 112*).

Music offers a five-fold service to liturgy (cf. *MS 5*)

1. Music helps to make prayer more attractive
The great musical tradition of the Church bears witness to her constant efforts to nourish faith by giving the arts a place in her worship (*SC 112*). In scripture (*Ex 15:20, 2 Chron 5:13*ff., *Eph 5:19, Col. 3:16*) and in the Fathers, (e.g. Augustine's *Confessions X, 33*) we find that music is a powerful means of instilling a desire for prayer. It is the hope of the Church today that the effective use of music will instil in the Christian a delight in celebrating the praise of God. (*General Instruction on Liturgy of the Hours,* 11 April 1971).

2. When we sing together we become more aware of the mystery of the liturgy
In the liturgy the Body of Christ, head and members, offers praise to the Father. (*SC 7*). A celebration in which priest, deacon, cantor, choir and congregation all sing the parts allocated to them shows forth the structure of the Christian

assembly as a community of praise in which certain members have particular services to perform. (*1.Cor. 12:48.*)

3. The singing of praise is the very bond of unity

Singing together is both an expression of unity and a powerful means of achieving it. "Who could retain a grievance against the man with whom he had joined in singing before God. The singing of praise is the very bond of unity" (*Ambrose*). When we sing together we are reminded that God has called us to be a single people dedicated to his praise.

4. The beauty of music raises our hearts to God

God's salvation comes to us in the liturgy through signs perceptible to the senses (*SC 7*). One of these signs is the beauty and solemnity which music brings to our worship. This does not mean that we should necessarily use complex and ornate forms of singing. The Church urges us to aim at worthy and religious celebration, a "noble simplicity" (*SC 34, MS 11*).

5. We echo on earth the heavenly hymn of praise

God invites us in the liturgy to taste on earth the gifts of the world to come (*Preface 68*). While present in this world we are not at home in it. We look forward to the heavenly liturgy which has been described to us by John in terms of song (*Rev 4:8*). When we sing in the liturgical assembly our voices blend with the choirs of angels and all the powers of heaven.

Criteria for the selection of music

1. Musical standards

Only music which is artistically and technically pleasing will enhance the liturgy with beauty. Trained musicians serve the liturgy by exercising judgment in this area.[1]

2. Musical style

The style of the music should suit the nationality, culture, age and mentality of the community. No kind of music is prohibited provided that it can truly give the liturgy a "more noble form" and that it respects the nature of each part of it (cf. *MS 9, SC 113*).

3. Degree of difficulty

The capacities of those who are to sing the music, whether choir, cantor or congregation, must be considered. If the choir is under strain because the music is too difficult, or if a setting of one of the people's chants is so difficult that only the choir can sing it, then this music is no longer serving the liturgy (*MS 9*).

4. Liturgical suitability

In the choice of music for the liturgy one must consider:

(a) the spirit of the celebration itself (*MS 9*) e.g. funeral, marriage, Easter, Lent.

(b) the varied roles that music will play within it e.g. acclamation, dialogue, meditation. (*IG 18*). The function of the singing determines the kind of singing.

(c) the fact that the sung parts will be thrown into relief; thus, the need to give preference to the more important parts (*IG 19*).

Instrumental music

The pipe organ is the traditional instrument of the Church. It is pre-eminently suitable for liturgical worship. Other instruments are welcomed into the liturgy provided that they can help the music to fulfil its ministerial function.

The instrumentalist can create an atmosphere conducive to

In the past, the worthiness or "sacredness" of music seemed a question of style, e.g. "The more it approaches in its movement, inspiration and savour the Gregorian form, the more sacred and liturgical it becomes" (Pius X: *Tra le Sol* 1903).

The Gregorian style was once quite ordinary and contemporary. While wishing to preserve the treasures of Gregorian chant, the Church urges us now to develop once again contemporary forms of music.

prayer by playing suitable music and thus encouraging "internal participation" (cf. *MS 15a*). For example, the use of instrumental music during the preparation of the gifts can keep this part of the Mass in its proper perspective relative to the more intense congregational involvement required for the Eucharistic Prayer. A festive voluntary at the end of the celebration is in keeping with the spirit of the dismissal: "The people return to their daily lives, praising and blessing God" (*Hippolytus*).

Preserving the heritage of sacred music

"The Church recognises Gregorian chant as being specially suited to the Roman liturgy. Therefore, other things being equal, it should be given pride of place in liturgical services" (*SC 116*).

In urging that vernacular languages be given a fitting place in the celebration of the liturgy the Church adds: "Provision should be made, however, to see that the faithful can also say or sing together in Latin those parts of the Ordinary of the Mass that concern them" (*SC 54*). In this connection Gregorian chant can be the bond joining great numbers of peoples into a single nation gathered together in the name of Christ with one heart, one mind, and one voice; for the movement towards unity, characterised by a concert of voices in a variety of languages, rhythms and melodies, displays in a remarkable way the agreement in diversity of the one Church" (cf. *Jubilate Deo*, Introduction).

The use of Latin chants in a vernacular celebration
Latin texts can still be used in vernacular celebrations. There is nothing to prevent different parts in one celebration being sung in different languages (*MS 51*). The simpler Gregorian chants promulgated by the Holy See in the booklet *Jubilate Deo* 1973, are intended to be congregational chants. It is hoped that local

churches will incorporate them into their own liturgies, and that at international gatherings the faithful of different languages may be able to sing together in Latin at least some parts of the Mass (*IG 19*).

Care should be taken that the use of Gregorian chant or polyphony does not exclude the people from participating in the parts of the Mass which belong to them. For example, since the *Sanctus* is an acclamation of the whole people, their silence during the singing of a polyphonic *Sanctus* by the choir cannot be harmonised with the pastoral celebration of the liturgy (cf. *MS 53*). It is for this reason that the *General Instruction on the Roman Missal* states that the easiest musical settings of the Latin texts should be used if congregational involvement is to be encouraged (*IG 19*).

However, at moments when the choir sings alone, polyphonic music can ideally express the spirit of the liturgy.

Gregorian chant in seminaries and novitiates

"In order to preserve the heritage of sacred music and genuinely promote the new forms of sacred singing, great importance is to be attached to the teaching and practice of music in seminaries, in the novitiates and houses of study of religious of both sexes, and also in other Catholic institutes and schools, especially in those higher institutes intended specially for this. Above all, the study and practice of Gregorian chant is to be promoted, because with its special characteristics it is a basis of great importance for the development of sacred music" (*MS 52*).

Appendix 1

AUDIBILITY IN LITURGICAL CELEBRATION: PUBLIC ADDRESS SYSTEM

One cannot over-emphasise the importance of audibility in the celebration of the liturgy. The Missal itself points out that "the nature of the presidential prayers demands that they be spoken in a loud and clear voice so that everyone present may hear and pay attention" (*IG 12*). No matter how good the texts may be, no matter how good the prayers, the homily, the comments, all is so much wasted effort if the speaker cannot be heard. In this connection we have a precedent from our Lord himself in the care he took to ensure that he would be heard and understood by the people of Galilee.

The following is taken by kind permission from *The Reading of the Word of God in Church* by the Dublin Diocesan Liturgical Commission:

Acoustics

When people complain that they cannot hear in church, it is usually not so much a problem of volume of sound as of unintelligibility. They hear sound but it is unintelligible. This unintelligibility is often caused by sound reflections off the many hard surfaces which make up the interior of traditional churches. Hard surfaces reflect sound much as a mirror reflects light, and since sound takes an appreciable time to travel, a person surrounded by hard surfaces hears the sound directly from the speaker's mouth, and then indirectly over and over again at different intervals of time as the sound is reflected back and forwards between the hard reflecting surfaces. In some churches a sound may be reflected around the building for as much as nine seconds, before it decays to inaudibility. During this time each new sound is overlaid and confused by the existing sounds still being reflected around the building.

Reverberation Time

The time it takes for a loud sound in an enclosed space to die to inaudibility is called reverberation time. Reverberation time of a radio talks studio is ideally .3 of a second. Reverberation time in some churches may be as much as 9 seconds. This is undesirable, because as stated in the above paragraph, it makes speech unintelligible.

The secret of designing a building for intelligible speech, is simply to provide sufficient absorbent surfaces which soak away sound quickly, so that even loud sounds will die away to nothing in as little as a quarter of a second.

New Churches

In the design of churches even to the present day, sufficient priority is still not being given to the vital necessity of designing a building which is suitable for speech. It is ludicrous, but true, that churches are still being built which are at best barely adequate for speech, and at worst totally unsuitable. In this matter, tradition, aesthetics and the needs even of church music must be subordinated to the primary function of designing a building in which the word of God can be comfortably heard.

There is a better appreciation today among architects of the need of acoustic considerations in designing churches, but is sufficient importance being attached to it? Acoustic consideration may mean a more expensive building, though not necessarily so, or at least more trouble for the architect, and some sacrifice in aesthetic values. For these reasons, even theoretically convinced of the importance of acoustics, architects do not usually employ acoustic consultants unless required to do so by a client.

Existing Churches

Many seem to be under the delusion that an acoustically poor church can be cured by the correct system of amplification. Priests frequently think in terms of changing the amplification system when they seek to improve intelligibility rather than tackling the real problem which is the acoustic quality of the building itself. With modern know-how and materials it is possible to materially improve the acoustic properties of a building in most, if not all, cases.

Amplification Systems

Speakers

Apart from different makes of amplification equipment, there are also different systems based on different principles. For instance the column speaker system seeks to control reverberation by beaming sound in different directions. The low-output system seeks to cut down reverberation by placing many speakers at a low level around the church. It may be helpful to some to know that speakers should not be erected too high from the floor level, the recommended height above floor level (by the firms who supply this system) is between six and a half to seven feet. With this system it is of vital importance to have the speakers very securely attached to their supports, to prevent removal by unauthorised persons.

The correct decision as to which system to use is dependent on the design of the *particular* church.

Microphone/Amplifier

To obtain the best results from any system, it is essential that only one microphone be in use at any one time, and that all other microphones, not in use, should be switched off, or the volume controls on the amplifier reduced to a minimum. Many installations which are basically good are not used to their best capacity, either because of a lack of knowledge of those in charge, or an unwillingness to spend the time controlling the amplifier. There are many parishioners who should be willing to undertake this task if they were asked. From time to time it is advisable to have someone in the church to check the volume and tone of the amplified voice, and send back word to the amplifier controller, if an alteration is necessary.

Types of Microphones

Halter or neck type microphones give very good results acoustically, but they are subject to continuous faults arising from wires becoming broken or disconnected from the microphone. Fixed or static microphones at the required locations are probably more satisfactory and serviceable. With the fixed microphone, greater freedom of movement can be obtained by using two or three of them at each of the three locations in the sanctuary, president's chair, ambo, and altar. For rapid and convenient adjustment, to suit the varying heights of those who are using them, a flexible adjustable metal holder for the microphone can be very useful. It should be remembered that the correct distance to speak from a microphone is from 9″ to 1′ 6″ depending upon the acoustic conditions prevailing.

The radio microphone has many advantages, not least among them being that it gives complete freedom of movement, and when suitable gives excellent results acoustically. Coupling this system with the fixed microphone can prove very successful.

It cannot be over-emphasised that professional advice is necessary when selecting an amplification system for a church, and one should certainly experiment with different systems, or maybe even a combination of systems before a final purchase is made.

Professional Advice

When seeking professional advice on the installation of an amplification system, it is desirable to ensure that the firm offers an after sales service. Some time ago the Communications Centre recommended that a fully qualified engineer be employed by them, appointed in consultation with the Institute of Engineers and the Institute of Architects. This engineer should be chosen because of his expertise in the theory and practice of acoustics. His functions would be:

(a) to be available as a consultant to any architect engaged in the country, in the building of schools and churches.

(b) to survey the churches of the country, diocese by diocese, and make reports to the bishops on the acoustic problems of particular churches; how they might be improved; and how much this might cost.

(c) to conduct a consumer survey of amplification systems, and advise on the most practical systems for practical applications.

Appendix 2

COMMUNION TWICE IN THE SAME DAY

According to the discipline currently in force, the faithful are permitted to receive Holy Communion a second time:[1]

On the evening of Saturday or of the day preceding a holyday of obligation, when they intend to fulfil the precept of hearing Mass, even though they have already received Holy Communion in the morning of that same day. At the second Mass of Easter and at one of the Masses celebrated on Christmas Day, even if they have already received Holy Communion at the Mass of the Paschal Vigil or at the midnight Mass of Christmas.

Likewise at the evening Mass of Holy Thursday, even if they have received Holy Communion at the earlier Mass of the Chrism.

Since, beyond these circumstances which have been mentioned, there are similar occasions which suggest that Holy Communion might fittingly be received twice in the same day, it is necessary here to determine more precisely the reasons for the new faculty.

The norm which the Church, a most provident mother, has introduced according to venerable custom and included in canon law by which the faithful are permitted to receive Holy Communion only once a day, remains intact, nor is it permitted

[1] *Immensae Caritatis*, 25 January 1973 (See translation in Flannery: *Vatican II* page 228f.)

to be set aside merely from motives of devotion. To a simple desire for repeated reception of Holy Communion it should be answered that the power of the sacrament by which faith, charity and the other virtues are nourished, strengthened and expressed is all the greater to the extent that one more devoutly approaches the sacred table. For, from the liturgical celebration the faithful should go out to the works of charity, piety and apostolic action so that "they may hold fast by their conduct and life to what they have received by faith and the sacrament".

Special circumstances, however, can occur when the faithful who have already received Holy Communion that same day, or even priests who have already celebrated Mass, may be present at some community celebration. They may receive Holy Communion again in the following instances:

(1) At those Masses in which the Sacraments of Baptism, Confirmation, Anointing of the Sick, Sacred Orders and Matrimony are administered; also at a Mass at which First Communion is received.

(2) At Masses at which a church or altar is consecrated; at Masses of religious profession or for the conferring of a "canonical mission".

(3) At the following Masses of the Dead: the funeral Mass, the Mass celebrated after notification of death, the Mass on the day of final burial and the Mass on the first anniversary.

(4) At the principal Mass celebrated in the cathedral or in the parish on the feast of Corpus Christi and on the day of a parochial visitation; at the Mass celebrated by the major superior of a religious community on the occasion of a canonical visitation, of special meetings or chapters.

(5) At the principal Mass of a Eucharistic or Marian Congress, whether international or national, regional or diocesan.

(6) At the principal Mass of any congress, sacred pilgrimage or preaching mission for the people.

(7) In the administration of Viaticum, in which communion can also be given to the relatives and friends of the patient.

(8) Also Local Ordinaries may, besides those cases mentioned above, grant permission *ad actum* to receive Holy Communion twice in the same day, as often as they shall judge it truly justified by reason of genuinely special circumstances, according to the norm of this Instruction.

Appendix·3

WHEN COMMUNION MAY BE RECEIVED UNDER BOTH KINDS[1]

At the bishop's discretion and after the necessary explanation, communion from the chalice is permitted for the following:

(1) adults at the Mass which follows their baptism; adults at the Mass in which they are confirmed; baptised persons who are being received into communion with the Church;

(2) the bride and bridegroom at their wedding Mass;

(3) the newly ordained at their ordination Mass;

(4) an abbess at the Mass in which she is blessed; virgins at the Mass of their consecration; professed religious, their parents and relatives, and members of their community at the Mass during which they make first or perpetual vows or renew their vows;

(5) lay missionaries at the Mass in which they publicly receive their mission; others at the Mass in which they receive an ecclesiastical mission;

(6) the sick person and all present when viaticum is administered at a Mass lawfully celebrated in the home;

(7) the deacon and ministers who exercise their office at a Mass with singing;

(8) when there is a concelebrated Mass:

(a) all, including the laity, who exercise a genuine liturgical function in the concelebration and also all seminarians who are present;

[1] Taken from *IG 242*.

(b) in their churches or oratories, all members of institutes which profess the evangelical counsels and other societies whose members dedicate themselves to God by religious vows, offering, or promise, as well as all those who live in the houses of such institutes and societies;

(9) priests who are present at large celebrations and are not able to celebrate or concelebrate;

(10) all who make a retreat or spiritual exercises, at a Mass specially celebrated for the participating group; all who take part in a meeting of a pastoral body, at a Mass celebrated in common;

(11) those listed in nos. 2 and 4, at Masses celebrating their jubilees;

(12) godparents, parents, wife or husband, and lay catechists of a newly baptised adult at the Mass of initiation;

(13) parents, relatives, and special benefactors who participate in the Mass of a newly ordained priest;

(14) members of communities at the conventual or community Mass, in accord with no. 76 of the *General Instruction of the Roman Missal.*

NB: In addition to the cases listed above, episcopal conferences may decide to what extent, for what motives, and in what conditions, ordinaries may concede communion under both kinds in other cases which have great importance for the spiritual life of a particular community or group of the faithful. (See *Sacramentali Communione,* 29 June 1970, translated in Flannery: *Vatican Council II,* pp.206 ff.)

Appendix 4

POSTURES AT MASS

The Episcopal Conference directs that the following postures be adopted by the faithful in the celebration of the Eucharist:

Introductory rites

Entrance	
Greeting	
Penitential Rite	STAND
Kyrie, Gloria	
Opening Prayer	

Liturgy of the Word

First Reading	
Responsorial Psalm	SIT
Second Reading	
Alleluia/Acclamation	
Gospel	STAND
Homily	SIT
Credo	
Prayers of the Faithful	STAND

Liturgy of the Eucharist

Preparation of the Gifts	
Orate Fratres	SIT
Prayer over the Gifts	

Eucharistic Prayer, from Preface to the Great Amen, inclusive (in special circumstances)	KNEEL or STAND
Communion rite from Our Father.	STAND
Prayer after Communion	STAND
(Notices)	SIT
Final greeting, blessing and dismissal	STAND

Bibliography

Prime sources with abbreviations used in text

General:

SC: *Sacrosanctum Concilium* Constitution on the Liturgy, 4 December 1963.

DV: *Dei Verbum* Dogmatic Constitution on Divine Revelation, 18 November 1965.

LG: *Lumen Gentium* Dogmatic Constitution on the Church, 21 November 1964.

PO: *Presbyterorum Ordinis* Ministry and Life of Priests, 7 December 1965.

ATE: *Ad Totam Ecclesiam* Directory Concerning Ecumenical Matters, 14 May 1967.

MS: *Musicam Sacram* Instruction on Music in the Liturgy, 5 March 1976.

All of the foregoing are translated in Flannery: *Vatican Council II*, Dominican Publications and Talbot Press, 1975. An invaluable work.

Baptism of Infants:

Ordo Baptismi Parvulorum Sacred Congregation for Divine Worship, 15 May 1969, with amendments in *Notitiae*, July-August 1973.

Rite of Baptism of Children Veritas Publications, July 1970. Referred to in *Directory* as *Rite* (*Rite of Baptism of Children*), *Introd* (*Introduction*) and *Gen. Introd.* (*General Introduction*).

Christian Initiation of Adults,
Rite of Initiation of Children of Catechetical Age,
Rite of Reception of Baptised Christians:

Ordo Initiationis Christianae Adultorum SCDW, 6 January 1972.
Rite of Christian Initiation of Adults ICEL draft translation.[1]
*Rite of Reception of Baptised Christians into Full Communion with
the Catholic Church* ICEL draft translation.

Confirmation:

Ordo Confirmationis SCDW, 22 August 1971.
The Rite of Confirmation Veritas 1975.

The Eucharist:

IG: *General Instruction on the Roman Missal* 26 March 1970.

EM: *Eucharisticum Mysterium* Instruction on the Worship of
the Eucharistic Mystery, 25 May 1967. Transl. Flannery op.
cit.

Missale Romanum SCDW, 26 March 1970.

The Roman Missal, Liturgical Books, 1974.

LI: *Liturgicae Instaurationes* Third Instruction on
Implementation of Liturgy Constitution, 5 September 1970.
Transl. Flannery op. cit.

EP: *Eucharistiae Participationem*, Letter on Eucharistic Prayers,
27 April 1973. Transl. Flannery, op. cit.

DG: *Decretum Generale quo Ritus Concelebrationis et
Communionis sub utraque specie promulgatur* 7 March 1965.
Transl. Flannery, op. cit.

RSCM: *Ritus Servandus in Concelebratione Missae*, 7 March
1965.

CM: *In Celebratione Missae* Concelebration, 7 August 1972.
Transl. Flannery, op. cit.

Directory on Children's Masses 1 November 1973. Transl.
Flannery, op. cit.

[1] ICEL, International Commission on English in the Liturgy, 1330,
Massachusetts Ave., NW, Washington DC 6005, USA.

Eucharistic Prayers for Children's Masses, Liturgical Books, 1976.

IMSG: *Instruction on Masses for Small Groups* 15 May 1969. Transl. Flannery, op. cit.

DSC: *De Sacri Communione et De Cultu Mysterii Eucharistici Extra Missam* 21 June 1973. Transl. ICEL.

Penance:

OP: *Ordo Paenitentiae* SCDW, 1974.

ID: *Indulgentiarum doctrina*, Const. Apost., Paul VI, 1 January 1967. AAS 59 (1967).

PAEN. *Paenitemini* AAS 58 (1966) 183.

Rite of Penance Veritas 1976.

Anointing and Pastoral Care of the Sick:

The Rite of Anointing and Pastoral Care of the Sick Liturgical Books 1974.

Ordination to the Priesthood:

Ordo of Ordination of Deacon, Priest and Bishop SCR 18 June 1968. Transl. by ICEL.

Marriage:

Ordo Celebrandi Matrimonium SCR, 19 March 1969.

The Celebration of Marriage Geoffrey Chapman 1971.

Christian Burial:

Ordo Exsequiarum SCDW 15 August 1969.

The Rite of Funerals Veritas Publications 1972.

Christian Burial Mount St. Anne's Liturgy Centre 1976.

Ministries of Lector, Acolyte: Deacon:

Ministeria Quaedam SCDW, 15 August 1972. Transl. in Flannery: *Vatican Council II* supra cit., pp. 427f.

Ordo of Institution of Readers and Acolytes SCDW, 3 December 1972. Transl. available from ICEL.

Ad Pascendum Apost. Letter giving norms for Order of Diaconate, 15 August 1972, Transl. Flannery, op. cit. pp. 443f.

Pontificalis Romani, Const. Apost. on Diaconate, 18 June 1968.

Ordo of Ordination of Deacon, Priest, Bishop SCDW 1968. Transl. from ICEL.

Music in the Liturgy

MS *Musicam Sacram* Instruction on Music in the Liturgy, 4 December 1963. Transl. in Flannery, op. cit., pp. 80f.